Pakistan History

Azhar ul Haque Sario

CONTENTS

1

Cultural Evolution

You know, Pakistan's culture is like a fascinating puzzle. It's got these ancient pieces from the Indus Valley civilization, you know, the folks who were building cities and making art way before many others. Then you've got the Islamic influence, which is like a whole other layer of the puzzle, adding beautiful mosques and shaping how people live their lives. And don't forget the British colonial era, which left its mark on everything from the government to the language.

It's pretty amazing to walk through a Pakistani bazaar and see all these different pieces fitting together. You might find an old building with intricate designs from the Indus Valley times, right next to a grand mosque that's centuries old. And then you'll see people using British-style road signs or speaking English, which is a leftover from the colonial days. It's like this crazy mix, but somehow it all works!

Now, let's take a little trip to Chitral. It's a beautiful place up in the mountains, and it's like a mini-Pakistan in terms of culture. You can see how the old ways of farming are still used, but then you also have modern roads and bridges that were built during the British times. And the people there, they're living their lives with a blend of traditional Islamic values and the rules that the British put in place. It's like a snapshot of how Pakistan's culture has evolved over time.

Let's dive deeper into the past. The Indus Valley civilization, that's where it all started. They were incredibly advanced for their time, with well-planned cities, beautiful art, and skilled craftsmanship. You can still see echoes of that in Pakistani culture today. But then, in the seventh century, Islam came to the region, and that changed everything. It brought a new religion, new architecture, and new ways of life. If you travel along the famous Khyber Pass or the Grand Trunk Road, you'll see historical sites that show just how much Islamic influence spread throughout the country.

And then, of course, there was the British colonial period. That's when things like the legal system and education were set up in a way that's still used today. It's interesting to see how Pakistani communities often blend these British-introduced systems with their traditional Islamic values. It's all part of the unique mix that makes Pakistan what it is.

Imagine this: You're walking through the ruins of Mohenjo-Daro, one of the ancient Indus Valley cities. You can almost picture the people who lived there thousands of years ago, going about their daily lives. Then you visit the Badshahi Mosque in Lahore, a majestic building that represents centuries of Islamic devotion and artistry. And as you wander through modern Pakistani cities, you notice the British-style buildings and the way people sometimes speak English. It's all part of the fascinating story of Pakistan's cultural journey.

Pakistan's culture isn't just about the past, though. It's a living, breathing thing that's constantly changing and evolving. It's like a river that's been fed by many different streams, each one adding its own unique flavor. And just like a river, it's always on the move, adapting to new challenges and opportunities.

Now, let's head up north to the Northern Areas of Pakistan. This is where you'll find some of the most breathtaking scenery in the world, but it's also a place where you can see the cultural mix in a whole new way. The landscape is rugged and varied, just like the different cultural influences that have shaped the region. You'll find ancient forts and villages nestled in the mountains, alongside remnants of British colonial architecture. It's like a living museum of Pakistan's history.

The people who live in the Northern Areas are incredibly diverse. You've got different ethnic groups, each with their own traditions and languages. And yet, they all live together in relative harmony, finding ways to bridge their differences. It's a testament to the resilience of Pakistani culture, its ability to adapt and evolve while still holding onto its core values.

So, what does all this mean for Pakistan today? Well, it means that the country is facing a unique set of challenges and opportunities. On the one hand, there's the constant tension between tradition and modernity. How do you preserve your cultural heritage while also embracing new ideas and technologies? On the other hand, there's the incredible diversity of the population. How do you create a sense of national unity when there are so many different ethnic groups and languages?

These are tough questions, but I think Pakistan is finding its own way to answer them. It's a country that's full of contradictions, but that's also what makes it so interesting. It's a place where the ancient and the modern, the traditional and the progressive, all come together to create something truly unique.

So, the next time you think of Pakistan, don't just think of the headlines you see in the news. Think of the rich tapestry of its culture, the way it's been shaped by thousands of years of history. Think of the bustling bazaars, the majestic mosques, the ancient ruins, and the modern cities. Think of the people, with their diverse languages, traditions, and beliefs. And think of the challenges they face, as well as the opportunities that lie ahead.

Pakistan is a country that's full of surprises, and its culture is no exception. It's a place where you can always expect the unexpected, and that's what makes it so fascinating. So, go ahead and explore it for yourself. You might just be amazed at what you find.

You know, Pakistan isn't just about mountains, valleys, and bustling cities. It's a country bursting with vibrant festivals and traditions that tell a story about its people, their history, and the bonds that hold them together. It's like a colorful tapestry woven with threads of joy, unity, and shared heritage.

Take Eid, for instance. It's not just a holiday; it's an explosion of emotions. Streets adorned with twinkling lights, houses filled with the aroma of delicious food, and families coming together to celebrate after a month of fasting. It's a time for forgiveness, sharing, and remembering those who are less fortunate. When you witness Eid in Pakistan, you understand how it strengthens the ties within communities and renews the spirit of togetherness.

And then there's Basant, the kite festival that paints the sky with a kaleidoscope of colors. It's a sight to behold! But it's more than just a visual spectacle; it's a social leveller. Rich or poor, young or old, everyone joins in the fun. The rooftops become battlegrounds for friendly kite duels, and the air buzzes with laughter and excitement. Basant shows us that even in the simplest of traditions, there's a power to bring people from all walks of life together.

But let's not forget the local harvest festivals, the unsung heroes of cultural expression. These celebrations may be smaller in scale, but they're no less significant. They connect people to the land, to their roots, and to the traditions that have been passed down through generations. Each region has its own unique way of marking the harvest, showcasing the diversity and richness of Pakistani culture. These festivals are like hidden gems, revealing the intricate details of the tapestry that is Pakistan.

Now, you might wonder, why are these festivals so important? Well, they're not just about having fun (although that's a big part of it!). They're about preserving heritage, passing down stories, and keeping traditions alive. They're about creating a sense of belonging, where everyone feels connected to something bigger than themselves. In a country as diverse as Pakistan, these festivals act as a unifying force, reminding people of their shared identity and values.

Think of it like this: Imagine a family gathering for a special occasion. Everyone has their own unique personality and quirks, but they all come together to share a meal, laugh, and make memories. Festivals are like that family gathering, but on a much larger scale. They bring entire communities together, fostering a sense of unity and pride in their shared heritage.

And let's not underestimate the power of these festivals to showcase Pakistan's vibrant culture to the world. Tourists flock to the country to witness the spectacle of Basant, the spiritual fervor of Eid, and the regional charm of harvest festivals. These events not only boost the local economy but also help to break down stereotypes and misconceptions about Pakistan. They show the world that this is a country with a rich and diverse cultural heritage, a place where tradition and modernity coexist harmoniously.

Of course, it's not always easy to preserve traditions in a rapidly changing world. Modernization and globalization pose challenges to age-old customs. But Pakistan is finding ways to adapt and evolve, while still holding onto its cultural roots. For example, many young people are embracing traditional music and dance forms, adding their own contemporary twists to keep them relevant. It's a beautiful example of how tradition can be a source of inspiration and innovation, rather than a barrier to progress.

In a nutshell, Pakistan's festivals and traditions are a testament to its resilience, creativity, and the enduring spirit of its people. They are not relics of the past but living, breathing expressions of identity that continue to shape and enrich the nation. So, the next time you hear about a festival in Pakistan, don't just dismiss it as a mere cultural curiosity. Take a closer look, and you might just discover a hidden world of meaning, connection, and joy.

Ever noticed how art speaks volumes about a place and its people? It's like a secret language that reveals their soul, their history, and the things they hold dear. In Pakistan, art forms like miniature painting, calligraphy, and music aren't just pretty things to look at or listen to; they're living, breathing reflections of the nation's vibrant spirit and rich heritage.

Let's start with miniature painting. Picture this: tiny, intricately detailed paintings on paper or cloth, bursting with color and telling stories from centuries ago. These aren't just pretty pictures; they're like windows into the past, showcasing the lives of kings and queens, epic battles, and everyday scenes. But it's not just about the past. Modern artists are using miniature painting to explore contemporary themes, keeping this ancient art form alive and relevant. It's a testament to the resilience of Pakistani culture, showing how it can adapt and evolve while still honoring its roots.

Then there's calligraphy, the art of beautiful writing. In Pakistan, calligraphy is more than just fancy lettering; it's a way to elevate words to a higher level, to turn them into works of art that touch the heart and soul. Whether it's verses from the Quran or poems about love and loss, calligraphy adds a layer of meaning and beauty to the written word. It's like a bridge between the spiritual and the everyday, reminding us that even simple words can have profound significance.

And of course, no discussion of Pakistani art would be complete without mentioning music. It's a diverse and vibrant landscape, ranging from classical ragas that transport you to another world, to modern fusions that blend traditional sounds with contemporary beats. Music is the heartbeat of Pakistani culture, a way for people to express their emotions, celebrate their joys, and mourn their losses. It's a language that everyone understands, regardless of their background or beliefs.

What's fascinating about these art forms is how they've evolved over time while still staying true to their roots. Miniature painting, for example, has seen changes in technique and subject matter, but it still retains the same level of detail and vibrancy that made it so popular centuries ago. Calligraphy has adapted to different scripts and styles, but its essence remains the same: to turn writing into an art form that inspires and uplifts. And music, well, it's always been a reflection of the times, but it always draws on the rich musical traditions that have been passed down through generations.

In a world that's constantly changing and becoming more homogenized, these art forms are like anchors, grounding people in their cultural identity. They're a way to connect with the past, to understand where you come from, and to appreciate the unique beauty of your own culture. They're also a way to express yourself, to tell your own stories, and to make your mark on the world.

Think of it like this: Imagine a family heirloom, passed down from generation to generation. It may have a few scratches and dents, but it's still cherished because of its history and the memories it holds. Pakistani art forms are like those heirlooms, carrying the weight of centuries of tradition and meaning. They're not just objects to be admired; they're living connections to the past, reminding us of who we are and where we come from.

But these art forms aren't just about the past; they're also about the future. They're a way to ensure that Pakistan's cultural heritage is not lost or forgotten in the rush of modernization. They're a way to inspire new generations of artists, musicians, and calligraphers, to keep the flame of creativity burning bright.

So, the next time you see a miniature painting, admire a piece of calligraphy, or listen to a Pakistani song, take a moment to appreciate the richness and depth of these art forms. They're more than just entertainment; they're a reflection of the soul of a nation, a testament to its resilience, creativity, and enduring spirit. They're a reminder that even in a world that's constantly changing, there are some things that remain timeless and precious.

Hey there, food lover! Let's talk about Pakistan, a country where the food isn't just about filling your belly—it's a whole experience that takes you on a wild ride through history, culture, and community. Imagine yourself strolling down the buzzing streets of Lahore, where the air is filled with the smoky aroma of sizzling kebabs. Or maybe you find yourself in a fancy dining room, savoring a biryani that's been passed down through generations, with roots tracing back to the grand Mughal kitchens.

Flavors of History and Community

Every dish in Pakistan has a story to tell. The street foods, like the tangy chaat or the crispy samosas, aren't just tasty snacks; they're like snapshots of everyday life. You'll see people from all walks of life huddled together, sharing these delicious treats and creating memories. On the other hand, those elaborate royal feasts, think nihari (a slow-cooked meat stew) or korma (a rich curry), are like time machines that transport you to the days of emperors and queens. These recipes have been passed down through centuries, carrying with them echoes of empires long gone.

But here's the thing: Pakistani food isn't just about individual experiences. It's about bringing people together, no matter where they come from or what their background is. It's like a giant potluck where everyone brings their unique flavors to the table. And when you take a bite, you're not just tasting the food; you're tasting the history, the culture, and the shared identity of an entire nation.

A Journey Through Pakistan's Culinary Landscape

Now, let's dive deeper into this culinary adventure. We'll explore how street food in cities like Karachi and Peshawar reflects the bustling energy of urban life, while dishes like biryani from Sindh and sarson ka saag (a mustard greens dish) from Punjab showcase the rich agricultural heritage of different regions. This culinary diversity isn't just about variety; it's about how different communities have come together to create a unique national identity. It's like a vibrant tapestry woven with threads of tradition, innovation, and communal spirit.

Imagine biting into a bun kebab in Karachi, a popular street food that bursts with flavor. It's more than just a meal; it's a symbol of the city's fast-paced lifestyle and the shared experiences of its people. Or picture yourself enjoying a plate of namak mandi (salt-cured meat) in

Peshawar, a dish that reflects the region's historical trade routes and cultural exchanges. These simple yet delicious street foods are the heart and soul of Pakistan's culinary scene.

But the culinary journey doesn't stop there. Let's move on to those grand royal feasts that are fit for a king or queen. Imagine the aroma of biryani wafting through the air, a dish that's been perfected over generations in Sindh. Or savor the earthy flavors of sarson ka saag from Punjab, a dish that's deeply rooted in the region's agricultural traditions. These elaborate feasts aren't just about indulging in rich flavors; they're about preserving centuries-old recipes and celebrating the cultural heritage of different communities.

The Unity in Diversity

What's fascinating about Pakistani cuisine is how it manages to celebrate both regional specialties and national staples. You'll find dishes like biryani and sarson ka saag being enjoyed across the country, transcending regional boundaries and creating a shared culinary experience. This culinary unity is a testament to the interconnectedness of Pakistan's diverse regions and the collective pride in its rich food heritage.

The diversity of Pakistani cuisine isn't just about different dishes; it's about different cooking techniques and ingredients that have been passed down through generations. Think about the art of cooking vegetables over an open flame or preparing raw snacks with fresh herbs and spices. These traditional practices are a testament to the ingenuity and resourcefulness of Pakistani cooks, who have managed to create delicious and nutritious meals using simple ingredients.

As you explore Pakistan's culinary landscape, you'll discover that food is more than just sustenance; it's a way of life. It's about family gatherings, community celebrations, and shared moments of joy.

Whether you're enjoying a quick bite at a street food stall or indulging in a lavish feast, you're partaking in a culinary tradition that's been shaped by centuries of history, culture, and community.

A Culinary Adventure Awaits

So, if you're ever in Pakistan, be sure to embark on a culinary adventure. Explore the bustling street food scenes, savor the flavors of regional specialties, and indulge in the grandeur of royal feasts. You'll discover that Pakistani cuisine is more than just food; it's a reflection of the country's soul, a celebration of its diversity, and a testament to its rich cultural heritage.

In the end, it's not just about what you eat; it's about the stories behind the dishes, the people you share them with, and the memories you create along the way. So, go ahead and take a bite of Pakistan—you won't be disappointed!

Food for Thought

As we conclude this culinary journey through Pakistan, let's take a moment to reflect on the profound impact that food has on our lives. It's not just about nourishment; it's about culture, community, and identity. It's about preserving traditions, celebrating diversity, and creating shared experiences.

So, the next time you sit down to a meal, take a moment to appreciate the rich history and cultural significance behind the dishes you're enjoying. Whether it's a simple home-cooked meal or a culinary masterpiece, remember that food is a powerful force that connects us all.

And if you ever have the chance to explore the culinary landscape of Pakistan, don't hesitate. It's a journey that will tantalize your taste buds, enrich your understanding of culture, and leave you with memories that will last a lifetime.

So, here's to the flavors of Pakistan—a culinary adventure that's as diverse and vibrant as the country itself.

2

Colonial Legacy

Hey there, let's dive into a captivating topic: how the shadows of British colonial rule still linger over Pakistan's courts and government, like echoes in a grand old building. It's a story of old laws, stubborn institutions, and the struggle to move forward.

Imagine walking into a courtroom in Pakistan today. You might feel like you've stepped back in time. The laws, the procedures, even the language used often hark back to the days of the British Raj. It's as if a piece of the past has been preserved, but not in a museum – it's in the very heart of the legal system.

You see, when the British ruled India (which included what is now Pakistan), they brought their own legal system along. This system, with its rules and regulations, was designed to serve the interests of the Empire. It's like a tailor making a suit for one person, but someone else tries to wear it years later – it's not going to fit quite right.

The same thing happened in Pakistan. After independence in 1947, the country kept much of the British legal framework. This made sense at the time – they needed a system to get things going. But as time passed, Pakistan changed, and its needs evolved. The old laws, however, didn't always keep pace.

One prime example of this is the Penal Code of 1860. This law, which deals with crimes and punishments, is still used in Pakistan today. It's like using an old map to navigate a modern city – some things might still be accurate, but others will lead you astray.

The problem is that this old Penal Code, and other similar laws, often clash with modern Pakistani society. They might not address new challenges like cybercrime or environmental issues. They might also contain outdated ideas about gender roles or social norms.

Now, you might be thinking, "Why not just change the laws?" Well, that's where things get tricky. Changing laws is like trying to rearrange furniture in a crowded room – you're bound to bump into something.

For starters, there's the issue of institutional inertia. This means that the courts and government agencies are used to working with the old laws. They know them inside out, like a chef knows their favorite recipe. Switching to new laws would be like asking that chef to suddenly cook a different cuisine – it would take time and effort to learn the new techniques.

Then, there are the vested interests. These are people or groups who benefit from the current system. It could be lawyers who specialize in the old laws, or politicians who use them to their advantage. They're like the people who have the best seats in the theater – they don't want to give them up.

All of this creates a kind of resistance to change. It's like a strong current pushing against any attempt to move forward. As a result, efforts to reform the legal system often get bogged down.

But it's not just about changing laws. It's also about changing mindsets. The way judges interpret the laws, the way lawyers argue their cases, the way people think about justice – all of these are shaped by the colonial legacy.

It's like a house that's been painted the same color for years. Even if you change the furniture inside, the walls still remind you of the old style. To truly modernize the legal system, you have to repaint those walls – change the underlying culture and way of thinking.

So, where does that leave Pakistan? Well, it's a bit of a mixed bag. There have been some efforts to update the laws, and there are many people pushing for reform. But the old colonial influences are still deeply ingrained.

It's like a tree with deep roots. You can trim the branches, but the roots remain. To truly change the tree, you have to dig deeper. That's the challenge facing Pakistan's legal system today.

It's a challenge, but it's not impossible. Other countries have gone through similar transformations. They've shed their colonial past and built legal systems that reflect their own values and needs. Pakistan can do the same.

But it won't be easy. It will require the combined efforts of lawyers, judges, lawmakers, and ordinary citizens. It will require a willingness to question old assumptions and embrace new ideas. It will require a commitment to building a legal system that is truly Pakistani, not just a copy of someone else's.

In the end, it's about more than just laws. It's about identity, justice, and the kind of society Pakistan wants to be. It's about finding its own voice in the world, not just echoing the voices of the past.

So, the next time you hear about a court case in Pakistan, or read about a new law being debated, remember this story. Remember the echoes of the past that still linger, and the ongoing struggle to build a legal system for the future. It's a story that's still unfolding, and it's one that we should all be paying attention to.

Alright folks, let's have a heart-to-heart about the education system in Pakistan. It's a fascinating story that's deeply intertwined with history, culture, and some lingering effects of British colonialism.

Ever noticed how in Pakistan, English seems to be the magic key to unlocking the best opportunities? Well, that's not by accident. It's a legacy of the British Raj, who ruled over the Indian subcontinent for many years.

Back then, they introduced a system of education that heavily emphasized English as the language of power and prestige.

The idea was to create a class of educated locals who could help them govern. But the unintended consequence was the creation of a sharp divide between the English-speaking elite and the rest of the population.

Fast forward to today, and you can still see this divide. Kids from wealthy families often go to fancy private schools where they learn everything in English. These schools have top-notch facilities, experienced teachers, and a curriculum that prepares students for international universities and high-paying jobs.

On the other hand, kids from less privileged backgrounds often end up in overcrowded public schools where the quality of education can be hit-or-miss. Many of these schools use Urdu or other local languages as the medium of instruction. This means that even bright students can struggle to compete with their English-speaking peers later in life.

It's like two separate worlds. The kids in the English-medium schools grow up with a sense of confidence and entitlement. They're groomed to be leaders, and they often end up holding top positions in government, business, and academia.

Meanwhile, the kids in the public schools often feel like they're playing catch-up. They might be just as smart, but they don't have the same advantages. This can lead to frustration, resentment, and a feeling of being left behind.

But it's not just about who gets the best jobs. It's also about cultural identity. When you prioritize one language over others, you're essentially saying that one culture is superior. This can lead to a loss of pride in one's own language and traditions.

Imagine growing up in a society where your mother tongue is seen as second-class. You might start to feel ashamed of your own culture, and you might try to assimilate into the dominant culture. This can lead to a sense of rootlessness and alienation.

So, what's the solution? Well, it's not easy. Changing an entire educational system is a massive undertaking. But there are some things that can be done.

For starters, we need to invest more in public education. This means improving facilities, training teachers, and creating a curriculum that is relevant to the lives of ordinary Pakistanis. It also means valuing local languages and incorporating them into the classroom.

We also need to challenge the idea that English is the only path to success. This means creating more opportunities for students who are educated in other languages. It means recognizing that intelligence and talent come in many forms, not just the ability to speak English.

And perhaps most importantly, we need to foster a sense of national unity. This means celebrating the diversity of Pakistan's cultures and languages. It means creating a society where everyone feels valued and respected, regardless of their background.

This is a long-term project, and it won't happen overnight. But it's essential if we want to create a more equitable and just society. It's about giving everyone the opportunity to reach their full potential, not just those who happen to speak the right language.

So, the next time you think about education in Pakistan, remember that it's not just about textbooks and exams. It's about power, culture, and identity. It's about the kind of society we want to build for ourselves and for future generations.

Let's not let the ghosts of colonialism haunt our education system any longer. Let's create a system that is truly Pakistani, one that celebrates our diversity and empowers all our citizens.

Alright folks, let's have a real chat about Pakistan's socioeconomic landscape. It's a country with a rich and complex history, but unfortunately, it's also one grappling with some deep-seated inequalities that have their roots in the colonial past.

Imagine a country where a small handful of people own most of the land and wealth, while the rest struggle to make ends meet. That's the reality in Pakistan, and it's not a coincidence. It's a direct result of policies put in place during the British colonial era, designed to benefit the ruling class at the expense of everyone else.

Think of it like a game of Monopoly, where some players start with a huge advantage. They own the best properties, collect the most rent, and have the power to shape the rules of the game. Meanwhile, the other players are stuck with scraps, struggling to survive.

In Pakistan, this "game" has been going on for generations. The land ownership patterns established during colonial times have created a system where a few families control vast estates, while millions of people are landless or have tiny plots that barely provide for their families.

This inequality isn't just about land, though. It's about power and privilege. The wealthy elite have the resources to influence politics, education, and the media. They can shape public opinion, manipulate laws, and protect their interests.

Meanwhile, the poor and marginalized are left out in the cold. They often lack access to basic services like healthcare and education. They're denied opportunities to participate in the political process and have their voices heard.

It's a vicious cycle. The rich get richer, the poor get poorer, and the gap between them grows wider and wider. This is not just an abstract problem – it affects the lives of millions of people every day.

Imagine trying to get ahead in a world where you're constantly held back. You're denied access to good schools, healthcare, and jobs. You're surrounded by poverty and despair. It's hard to stay hopeful and motivated when the deck is stacked against you.

But it's not just about individual struggles. This inequality also has a profound impact on society as a whole. It breeds resentment, division, and conflict. It undermines social cohesion and makes it harder to build a strong and prosperous nation.

So, what can be done? Well, it's not going to be easy. These inequalities are deeply entrenched and have been reinforced over generations. But that doesn't mean we should give up.

The first step is to acknowledge the problem. We need to recognize that the current system is unfair and unsustainable. We need to have honest conversations about the legacy of colonialism and its impact on Pakistani society.

We also need to challenge the power of the elite. This means reforming laws and regulations that favor the wealthy. It means creating a level playing field where everyone has a fair chance to succeed.

It also means investing in education and healthcare for all. This is not just a matter of social justice, it's also a matter of economic sense. A healthy and educated population is a more productive and prosperous one.

And perhaps most importantly, we need to build a sense of national unity. This means recognizing the diversity of Pakistani society and celebrating the contributions of all its citizens. It means creating a society where everyone feels valued and respected, regardless of their social status.

This is a long-term project, and it won't happen overnight. But it's essential if we want to build a better future for Pakistan. It's about creating a society that is fair, just, and inclusive.

It's not just about fixing the past, it's about building a better future. A future where everyone has the opportunity to thrive, regardless of their background. A future where Pakistan can truly live up to its potential as a great nation.

Let's not let the ghosts of colonialism hold us back any longer. Let's create a new chapter in Pakistan's history, one that is defined by equality, opportunity, and justice for all.

Let's have a heart-to-heart about the legacy of British rule in Pakistan, a tale that goes deeper than just red coats and tea parties. The British left more than just their buildings and infrastructure; they left a way of thinking, a set of values, a cultural echo that still resonates today.

Imagine this: You're a kid in Pakistan, growing up in the shadow of the British Raj. You go to school and everything is taught in English, a language you barely understand. The books you read are filled with stories of British heroes and explorers. You're told that your own culture, your own language, is somehow inferior.

This was the reality for generations of Pakistanis. The British, with their stiff upper lips and their air of superiority, managed to instill a sense of cultural inferiority in the people they ruled. It was a subtle form of brainwashing, one that had a lasting impact.

Even after Pakistan gained independence in 1947, this sense of cultural inferiority lingered. English remained the language of power, the language of the elite. It was the key to getting a good education, a good job, a good life.

This created a divide in society, a hierarchy based on language. Those who spoke English fluently were seen as more intelligent, more sophisticated, more worthy. Those who didn't were often marginalized and looked down upon.

This linguistic divide was just the tip of the iceberg. British cultural hegemony extended to other areas as well. They introduced Western educational models that emphasized individualism and secularism, which clashed with traditional Pakistani values that emphasized community and religion.

Imagine being told that your way of life, the way your ancestors lived for centuries, is somehow backward or outdated. This can lead to a sense of cultural dissonance, a feeling of being caught between two worlds.

The British also introduced their own social norms and customs, which were often at odds with Pakistani traditions. This created a sense of confusion and insecurity, as people tried to navigate these conflicting values.

It's like being invited to a party where you don't know the rules. You're not sure how to dress, what to say, or how to behave. You feel like an outsider, like you don't belong.

This is the legacy of British cultural hegemony in Pakistan. It's a legacy that continues to shape Pakistani identity and social dynamics even today. It's seen in the way people speak, the way they dress, the way they interact with each other.

It's also seen in the way Pakistanis view themselves and their place in the world. Many still suffer from a lingering sense of inferiority, a feeling that their own culture is not as good as the West.

This internalized colonialism is a serious problem. It can lead to a lack of self-confidence, a lack of pride in one's own culture, and a desire to emulate Western ways.

But it's not all doom and gloom. There's a growing movement in Pakistan to reclaim its cultural heritage, to celebrate its unique identity. This is seen in the resurgence of traditional music and dance, the revival of indigenous languages, and the growing interest in Pakistani history and culture.

It's a long and difficult process, but it's a necessary one. Pakistan needs to shed the shackles of its colonial past and embrace its own unique identity. It needs to recognize that its culture is just as valuable, just as worthy, as any other.

This is not just about the past. It's about the future. It's about creating a society that is confident, self-assured, and proud of its heritage. It's about building a Pakistan that is truly independent, not just in name but in spirit.

So, let's have a conversation about the legacy of British cultural hegemony in Pakistan. Let's acknowledge the damage that it has done, but let's also celebrate the resilience and strength of Pakistani culture.

Let's work together to build a Pakistan that is free from the shadows of the past, a Pakistan that is confident in its own skin, a Pakistan that is truly its own.

3

Partition Trauma

Imagine for a moment the chaos and fear of 1947. The Partition of Pakistan was a seismic event, ripping apart families, communities, and lives. It was a time of unimaginable hardship, but amidst the darkness, there were stories of incredible courage and resilience.

Let me tell you about these people, ordinary folks who found themselves in extraordinary circumstances. They were farmers, teachers, shopkeepers - people just like you and me. Suddenly, their world turned upside down. They lost their homes, their loved ones, and everything they held dear.

You might think that such a trauma would break a person, and in some ways, it did. But it also brought out a hidden strength, a resilience that many didn't even know they had. These were people who had every reason to give up, yet they refused to succumb to despair.

One woman, a young mother at the time, told me how she fled her village with just her children and the clothes on her back. They walked for days, facing hunger, thirst, and the constant fear of violence. But she never gave up hope. She knew she had to survive for her children.

Eventually, they reached a refugee camp, where they started to rebuild their lives. It wasn't easy. They had nothing, but they had each other. Slowly, they built a new home, a new community. The woman found work as a seamstress, stitching together not just clothes but the torn fabric of her life.

This story isn't unique. I've heard countless tales of similar courage and determination. People who lost everything found ways to start over. They turned their pain into purpose, their loss into resilience. They showed us that the human spirit is a powerful thing, capable of enduring even the darkest of times.

Take the example of a young man who lost his family in the violence. He was filled with anger and grief, but he channeled those emotions into helping others. He became a volunteer at a refugee camp, providing food and shelter to those who had lost everything. In the process, he found a sense of meaning and purpose that helped him heal.

These stories aren't just about survival; they're about transformation. The Partition forced people to adapt, to change, and in many cases, to become stronger and more resilient than they ever thought possible. It was a time of immense upheaval, but it was also a time of incredible growth.

One thing that strikes me about these narratives is the importance of community. In the face of such widespread displacement and loss, people came together to support each other. They formed new communities, sharing resources, skills, and above all, hope. They reminded each other that they were not alone, that together they could overcome even the most daunting challenges.

Another common thread is the power of faith. For many, their faith was a source of strength and solace during this difficult time. It gave them a sense of meaning and purpose, a reason to keep going even when everything seemed lost.

Of course, not everyone found resilience. Some were overwhelmed by grief and despair. But even in these stories, there are glimmers of hope. There are tales of kindness and compassion, of strangers helping strangers, of shared humanity amidst the chaos.

It's important to remember that these stories are not just historical anecdotes. They have relevance today. The world is still full of conflict and upheaval, and people are still being displaced and traumatized. But these stories from the Partition remind us that even in the darkest of times, there is hope. There is resilience.

We can learn a lot from these survivors. They teach us that even when everything seems lost, it's possible to find a way forward. They show us that the human spirit is incredibly strong and that we are capable of more than we often think.

So, the next time you hear about a conflict or disaster in the news, remember the stories of the Partition survivors. Remember their courage, their resilience, and their unwavering determination to rebuild their lives. Their stories are a testament to the strength of the human spirit, a reminder that even in the face of adversity, there is always hope.

Picture this: 1947, the Indian subcontinent is in chaos. The partition of Pakistan is tearing through communities, leaving behind a trail of violence and displacement. It's a historical wound that's still bleeding, even today.

Think about it like this: Imagine a family living in a house that gets split in two. Some members are forced to move, while others stay behind. There's anger, resentment, and a sense of loss that lingers long after the walls have been put up.

That's what happened during the partition. Families were torn apart, friendships were shattered, and communities were divided along religious lines.

The scars of that event are still visible in Pakistan's society, manifesting in ongoing violence, distrust, and a lack of unity.

Let's not sugarcoat it: the partition was a tragedy. It was a time of unimaginable pain and suffering, and its impact is still felt today. But if we want to move forward as a nation, we need to acknowledge this painful past and find ways to heal.

So, what can we do? Well, for starters, we need to address the historical grievances that continue to fuel the fire of division. We need to have open and honest conversations about what happened and why it happened. We need to acknowledge the pain and suffering that people experienced on both sides of the divide.

But it's not just about talking; it's also about action. We need to implement policies that promote unity and reconciliation. We need to celebrate our diversity and create opportunities for people from different backgrounds to come together and build trust.

Think about it like this: Imagine two neighbors who have been feuding for years. The only way they can move forward is to sit down, talk things out, and find common ground. Maybe they'll never be best friends, but they can learn to coexist peacefully.

That's the kind of approach we need in Pakistan. We need to find ways to bridge the divides that have been created by history and build a future where everyone feels like they belong.

It won't be easy, and it won't happen overnight. But it's essential if we want to create a truly united and prosperous Pakistan. We need to move beyond the old narratives of division and create a new story, one that celebrates our shared humanity and our common aspirations.

So, how do we do this? Well, there's no one-size-fits-all answer, but here are a few ideas:

Education: We need to teach our children about the partition in a way that's honest and unbiased. We need to help them understand the complex historical context and the human cost of the conflict.

Interfaith dialogue: We need to create spaces where people of different faiths can come together and learn from each other. This can help to break down stereotypes and build bridges of understanding.

Cultural exchange: We need to celebrate the rich diversity of Pakistan's culture and heritage. This can help to foster a sense of shared identity and pride.

Economic development: We need to create opportunities for all Pakistanis, regardless of their background or ethnicity. This can help to reduce poverty and inequality, which are often drivers of conflict.

These are just a few suggestions, and there are many other ways we can work towards reconciliation and unity. The most important thing is that we start somewhere. We can't let the ghosts of the past continue to haunt us. We need to break the cycle of violence and mistrust and build a future where all Pakistanis can live in peace and harmony.

Let's face it: we have a long way to go. The wounds of partition are still raw, and the challenges we face are immense. But we can't give up hope. We need to believe in the power of change and the resilience of the human spirit.

Remember, we are all Pakistanis. We share a common history, a common culture, and a common destiny. It's time for us to put aside our differences and work together to build a better future for ourselves and our children.

The partition may have divided us, but it doesn't have to define us. We have the power to write a new chapter in our history, one that's filled with hope, healing, and unity. Let's make it happen.

Picture this: 1947, the partition of Pakistan. Imagine the chaos, the heartbreak, the sheer terror as millions of people are uprooted from their homes, forced to flee to a new land. These refugees faced unimaginable hardship and loss, their stories often lost in the grander narrative of history. But their journeys weren't just about survival; they were about resilience, about rebuilding, and about contributing to their new homeland in remarkable ways.

Think of it like a seed blown by the wind, landing in a new and unfamiliar soil. At first, it might struggle to take root, but with time and perseverance, it can grow into something beautiful and strong. That's what happened with the refugees of partition. They faced adversity head-on, and in the process, they helped to shape the very fabric of Pakistan.

You see, these refugees weren't just victims. They were survivors, they were entrepreneurs, they were innovators. They brought with them a wealth of skills and experiences that proved invaluable in rebuilding a shattered nation.

For instance, many refugees were skilled artisans and craftsmen. They set up shops and businesses, creating jobs and boosting the economy. Others were farmers, who helped to cultivate the land and feed the growing population. Some were teachers and doctors, who provided essential services to their new communities.

But their contributions went beyond just the practical. These refugees also brought with them a rich cultural heritage, a diversity of languages, traditions, and customs that enriched Pakistani society. Their food, music, and art became part of the national identity, a testament to their resilience and their ability to adapt and thrive in a new environment.

Take the city of Karachi, for example. It was transformed by the influx of refugees, who brought with them a spirit of enterprise and innovation. They built businesses, established industries, and turned Karachi into a bustling metropolis, the economic heart of Pakistan.

In Lahore, the refugees revitalized the city's cultural scene, establishing theaters, art galleries, and literary circles. They brought with them a love of learning and a thirst for knowledge, which helped to shape Pakistan's intellectual and academic landscape.

These are just a few examples of the many ways in which refugees contributed to Pakistani society. Their stories are a testament to the human spirit's ability to overcome adversity and to find hope and opportunity in the most difficult of circumstances.

But for too long, these stories have been overlooked or marginalized. We tend to focus on the pain and suffering of partition, and rightfully so. But we also need to acknowledge the resilience and the contributions of those who were displaced. We need to recognize their role in building the Pakistan we know today.

By understanding their stories, we can gain a deeper appreciation for the diversity and resilience of our nation. We can learn from their experiences and draw inspiration from their courage. And we can honor their legacy by continuing to build a Pakistan that is inclusive, tolerant, and welcoming to all.

So, the next time you hear about refugees, remember the stories of those who came to Pakistan during partition. Remember their struggles, their resilience, and their contributions. Their stories are not just a footnote in history; they are an integral part of our national narrative. They remind us that even in the face of adversity, there is always hope, there is always a way forward. And that's a message we all need to hear.

Imagine, if you will, a family tree where each branch represents a generation. Now imagine a storm ripping through this tree, leaving behind broken limbs and scattered leaves. That's what the partition of Pakistan in 1947 was like for countless families. It was a traumatic event that left deep scars, not just on those who lived through it, but on their children, their grandchildren, and even their great-grandchildren.

These scars aren't physical, of course. They're etched into the soul, passed down through stories whispered around kitchen tables, through songs sung at family gatherings, and through rituals observed generation after generation. It's a collective trauma that's become woven into the very fabric of Pakistani society, shaping its cultural practices and influencing how different communities interact with each other.

Think about it like this: when you experience something truly terrible, it doesn't just go away. It stays with you, lurking in the shadows of your mind, influencing your thoughts and behaviors in ways you may not even realize. And when you share those experiences with others, when you pass them down to your children and grandchildren, they too carry a piece of that trauma.

That's what happened in Pakistan after the partition. The violence, the displacement, the loss – it all became a part of the collective memory, a shared burden carried by generations. It's like a ghost that haunts the family home, its presence felt even though it's never seen.

But how exactly does this trauma manifest itself? Well, it's subtle, often hidden beneath the surface of everyday life. It might be a lingering mistrust between different communities, a reluctance to talk about certain events, or a particular way of celebrating festivals or commemorating important dates.

For example, many families have stories about the partition that have been passed down through the generations. These stories often recount the horrors of violence and displacement, but they also celebrate the resilience and courage of those who survived. They're a way of remembering the past, of honoring those who came before, and of instilling a sense of identity and belonging in younger generations.

Similarly, communal rituals and gatherings often serve as a way to process and share this collective trauma. For instance, during Muharram, the Shi'a community mourns the martyrdom of Imam Hussain, a historical event that resonates deeply with the suffering experienced during partition. These rituals offer a space for communal healing and a way to connect with a shared past.

But the influence of partition goes beyond family stories and religious rituals. It's also evident in Pakistani cinema and literature, which often grapple with themes of displacement, loss, and identity. These cultural representations reflect the ongoing struggle to come to terms with a traumatic past, to find meaning in the midst of suffering, and to forge a new sense of identity in the aftermath of tragedy.

This complex interplay between memory, identity, and trauma is not unique to Pakistan. It's a phenomenon seen in many societies that have experienced large-scale violence or displacement. But in Pakistan, the partition has a particular resonance, a particular power to shape the way people see themselves and their communities.

It's important to understand this dynamic because it has a profound impact on contemporary social relationships and inter-community dynamics. The trauma of partition is not just a historical event; it's a living reality that continues to shape the present. It influences how people perceive each other, how they interact, and how they understand their place in society.

Acknowledging this legacy of trauma is not about dwelling on the past or perpetuating feelings of victimhood. It's about understanding the roots of our present challenges and finding ways to heal and move forward. It's about recognizing the resilience of those who came before us and drawing inspiration from their courage and determination.

By understanding the impact of partition on generational identity, we can begin to create a more inclusive and tolerant society, one that recognizes the diversity of our experiences and embraces the common humanity that binds us all. It's a long and difficult journey, but it's a journey worth taking. Because ultimately, healing the wounds of the past is the key to building a better future for all Pakistanis.

4

Independence Struggles

Ever heard the saying, "There's more to the story than meets the eye?" Well, that's absolutely true when it comes to Pakistan's fight for freedom. We all know the big names – Muhammad Ali Jinnah and Mahatma Gandhi – but let's be honest, focusing only on them is like watching a movie trailer and missing the whole film.

There's a whole cast of unsung heroes, ordinary people, and local communities whose sweat and tears were just as important. Their stories are tucked away in the footnotes of history, waiting to be discovered. It's time to shine a light on these forgotten heroes because their contributions were essential to Pakistan's journey towards independence.

Think of it like this: Imagine a massive puzzle representing Pakistan's freedom struggle. The big pieces with Jinnah and Gandhi are obvious, right? But it's the smaller, unique pieces that truly complete the picture. These are the stories of grassroots organizers, local resistance fighters, writers, and ordinary folks who, together, made a massive difference.

Let's take Reverend Robert Caldwell, for example. This guy wasn't a household name, but he was a force to be reckoned with. He loudly opposed British military control and passionately fought for the rights of those pushed to the sidelines. His story shows us that the fight for freedom wasn't just happening in the political arena; it was a mosaic of people from all walks of life standing up for what they believed in.

And then there were the local communities. These weren't just groups of people; they were the heart and soul of the independence movement. They organized protests, spread messages against colonial rule, and even provided safe havens for those on the run. It was their unwavering determination that kept the fire of freedom burning.

Now, let's talk about some other amazing folks you might not have heard of. The author of "Tarana-e-Milli," a powerful poem that stirred national pride, played a huge role in uniting people for the cause. Literature like this wasn't just words on paper; it was fuel for the revolution.

But it wasn't just writers – entire towns and villages joined the fight. They resisted in their own ways, sometimes quietly, sometimes loudly. Picture secret meetings, smuggled messages, and everyday people risking their safety to help the cause. These actions might seem small, but together, they created a tidal wave of resistance that couldn't be ignored.

Now, here's the thing: when we dig deeper into these stories, we realize that Pakistan's independence wasn't a simple story with just a few heroes. It was a messy, beautiful, complicated journey filled with countless acts of courage and sacrifice.

Think of it like a giant tapestry – each thread, no matter how small, contributes to the overall design. The stories of these unsung heroes are the threads that weave together the rich, textured history of Pakistan.

When we acknowledge these contributions, we're not just filling in the gaps of history; we're giving credit where it's due. We're honoring the memories of those who might not have made it into the history books but whose actions were just as important as those of the big-name leaders.

And here's the kicker: by understanding the full picture, we gain a deeper appreciation for the complexities and struggles that led to Pakistan's independence. It's like finally seeing the full picture of that puzzle we talked about earlier.

So, the next time you hear about Pakistan's fight for freedom, remember that it wasn't just a story of a few famous figures. It was a symphony of countless voices, each playing their part to create a harmonious melody of freedom.

The stories of these unsung heroes remind us that even small actions can have a massive impact. They show us that ordinary people can achieve extraordinary things when they stand together for a common cause.

So, let's keep exploring these hidden chapters of history. Let's celebrate the everyday people who dared to dream of a free Pakistan and worked tirelessly to make that dream a reality. Their stories deserve to be heard, their contributions deserve to be recognized, and their legacies deserve to be cherished. Because in the end, it's the collective spirit of a nation that truly defines its journey towards freedom.

Imagine a group of passionate individuals, united by a shared vision of freedom, coming together to challenge the mighty British Empire. Sounds like a scene from a movie, right? But this was the reality in Pakistan, where grassroots movements like the Khilafat Movement and the All India Muslim Students Federation (AIMSF) played a massive role in the country's journey towards independence.

Now, you might be thinking, "Grassroots movements? Don't those usually involve planting trees and saving the environment?" Well, in this case, they planted seeds of resistance and saved a nation from colonial rule! These movements weren't about armed rebellion or violent protests; instead, they used a different set of tools:

Nonviolent Resistance: Think of it like a peaceful protest, but on a massive scale. These movements organized boycotts, strikes, and demonstrations that disrupted the British administration and made it clear that the people wouldn't be silenced. It was like a wave of peaceful defiance washing over the country.

Mass Mobilization: The key to their success was getting everyone on board, from religious leaders to students, to farmers. They used speeches, pamphlets, and even songs to rally the masses and create a sense of unity. It was like a giant pep rally for freedom!

Political Advocacy: They didn't just make noise; they also made demands. They used their growing influence to push for reforms and greater representation for Muslims in the political system. It was like a persistent knocking on the door of power, demanding to be heard.

The Khilafat Movement, initially focused on protecting the Ottoman Caliphate, quickly evolved into a broader movement for independence. It united Muslims from all walks of life under a common cause, showcasing the power of shared faith and purpose.

Meanwhile, the AIMSF tapped into the energy of the youth. They organized educational programs and debates, turning students into passionate advocates for freedom. It was like a classroom turned into a battleground for ideas, with young minds hungry for change.

These movements weren't just about tearing down colonial rule; they were about building something new. They laid the foundation for a future independent nation by fostering a sense of national identity and instilling a spirit of resistance in the hearts of the people.

Think of it like building a house: The Khilafat Movement and AIMSF laid the foundation, providing the solid base upon which the structure of an independent Pakistan could be built. Their efforts were the building blocks of a nation.

But how did they achieve all this? Well, they were masters of organization. They had a clear vision and a well-structured plan. They built networks, mobilized resources, and communicated their message effectively. It was like a well-oiled machine, with every part working in harmony to achieve a common goal.

Of course, it wasn't always smooth sailing. They faced opposition, repression, and even violence from the colonial authorities. But they never gave up. Their resilience and determination were truly inspiring. It was like a David vs. Goliath story, with the underdog refusing to back down.

The impact of these movements was undeniable. They weakened the British Raj and made it clear that their days were numbered. They also created a sense of hope and possibility among the people, proving that even the most powerful empires can be challenged. It was like a crack in a dam, slowly widening until it could no longer hold back the flood of change.

The legacy of the Khilafat Movement and the AIMSF lives on in Pakistan's vibrant civil society and political landscape. Their example reminds us that ordinary people can achieve extraordinary things when they unite for a common cause. It's a testament to the power of grass-roots movements and the enduring spirit of human resilience.

So, the next time you hear about Pakistan's independence, remember that it wasn't just the story of Jinnah and Gandhi. It was also the story of countless unsung heroes who fought for freedom in their own way. Their stories might not be as well-known, but their contributions were just as important.

These movements weren't just about historical events; they offer valuable lessons for us today. They teach us the power of nonviolence, the importance of unity, and the unwavering spirit needed to overcome oppression. They show us that change is possible, even in the face of seemingly insurmountable odds.

So, let's celebrate the unsung heroes of Pakistan's independence struggle. Let's remember their courage, their resilience, and their unwavering belief in a better future. Their stories inspire us to fight for justice, equality, and a world where everyone's voice is heard.

And who knows, maybe their example will inspire us to create our own grassroots movements for positive change. After all, as history has shown us, the power to shape our destiny lies not just in the hands of a few leaders, but in the hearts of the many who dare to dream of a better world.

Imagine this: A time when a new country was being born, and not everyone agreed on how it should be done. This is the story of Pakistan's fight for independence, a story where women often get left in the shadows. But their part in it was HUGE, way more than just cheering from the sidelines.

These women were brave, stepping up when it was risky, and facing the same dangers as the men.

They organized rallies, stood up to the authorities, and even treated wounded fighters when no one else would. These weren't just ordinary actions; they were bold statements that women deserved a place in the fight for their country's future.

One of the most famous figures is Fatima Jinnah, who earned the title "Mother of the Nation." She wasn't just a symbol; she was a real leader, advising those in charge and inspiring regular people to get involved. Her voice was powerful and persuasive, helping to unite a divided country behind the dream of independence.

But it wasn't just the famous women who made a difference. Countless others worked behind the scenes, educating people about their rights, providing crucial support to the movement, and keeping the spirit of resistance alive. They might not be in history books, but their contributions were just as important.

These women were changing more than just a political situation; they were changing how society saw them. By taking on roles that were usually reserved for men, they were breaking down old-fashioned ideas and showing everyone that women could lead, too. They were fighting for a Pakistan where everyone, no matter their gender, could have a say and contribute to the nation's future.

Their courage and determination weren't just about winning independence; they were about building a new country based on equality and inclusion. This was a vision of Pakistan where diversity was celebrated and everyone had the chance to shine. These women were not just fighting for freedom from a foreign power; they were fighting for freedom from old ways of thinking.

So, what did all this mean for Pakistan? Well, it's like a ripple effect. When these women stepped up, they sent a message that echoed through generations. They showed that progress doesn't happen by accident; it takes people working together, regardless of their gender or background. Their legacy is the idea that every single person in Pakistan has the power to make a difference, and that's a pretty amazing thing.

Now, let's dig a little deeper. These women weren't just involved; they were essential. Think about it: when the men were fighting, who was taking care of everything else? Women were running households, raising families, and keeping communities together. Without their support, the whole independence movement could have fallen apart.

The bravery of these women is almost hard to imagine. They were risking their lives, their homes, and their families for the cause. Imagine being a woman in those days, expected to stay out of politics and focus on home life, and then making the decision to march in a protest, or hide a freedom fighter from the authorities. That takes guts!

And leadership wasn't just about giving speeches; it was about making tough choices and guiding others through uncertain times. Fatima Jinnah did this with incredible skill, earning the respect of people from all walks of life. Her ability to connect with people on a personal level helped to inspire and motivate them, even when things looked bleak.

But let's not forget those unsung heroes, the women whose names might not be known but whose actions spoke volumes. They were the ones who taught others about the importance of independence, who organized local groups, and who kept the momentum going when it seemed like the fight was lost. Their contributions were the backbone of the entire movement.

The most inspiring thing about these women is that they weren't just fighting for themselves; they were fighting for future generations. They knew that a free Pakistan wasn't just about political independence; it was about social and cultural change. They wanted a country where girls could get an education, where women could have careers, and where everyone had the chance to reach their full potential.

Their resilience in the face of overwhelming odds is a lesson for us all. They didn't give up, even when things got tough. They kept pushing forward, believing in a better future for their country. And in the end, their efforts paid off.

So, what can we learn from all this? Well, first of all, we need to give these women the credit they deserve. Their stories should be taught in schools, celebrated in public, and remembered as part of Pakistan's national identity. We need to understand that the country we have today wouldn't exist without their sacrifices.

But it's not just about the past; it's about the future. The spirit of those women should continue to inspire us to fight for a more just and equitable society. We need to embrace diversity, challenge outdated norms, and work together to create a Pakistan where everyone has the chance to thrive.

Think about it: if these women could achieve so much under such difficult circumstances, what could we accomplish today with all the resources and opportunities we have? The answer is anything we set our minds to. The legacy of these brave women is a reminder that change is always possible, as long as we have the courage to fight for it.

In short, the women of Pakistan's independence movement weren't just participants; they were catalysts for change. Their bravery, leadership, and resilience shaped the country in ways that are still felt today.

Their story is a testament to the power of ordinary people to achieve extraordinary things when they unite behind a common goal. Let's remember their legacy and continue their fight for a brighter future for Pakistan.

Ever heard the saying, "There's always more than meets the eye?" That couldn't be truer when we talk about Pakistan's journey to independence. You see, history books often love highlighting the big names and famous events, but there's a whole bunch of folks who get left out of the spotlight. And guess what? Their stories are just as important, maybe even more so.

We're talking about women, religious minorities, folks who weren't well off... these are the groups who often get swept under the rug when the story of Pakistan is told. But if you really want to understand how this nation came to be, you've got to hear their side of things.

Let's start with the women. They weren't just sitting around while the men fought for freedom. They were right in the thick of it, marching in protests and even organizing their own. But that's not all. They were also holding down the fort at home, taking care of families and communities while the country was in chaos. Imagine trying to keep things running smoothly when everything around you is falling apart!

Religious minorities were another group who faced their own unique challenges. Imagine being a Christian or Hindu in a country that was becoming a homeland for Muslims. They could have easily been pushed aside, but instead, they chose to stay and contribute. They spoke up for their rights, fought for a place in the new society, and even tried to bridge the gap between different communities. Talk about resilience!

And then there were the folks who weren't wealthy or powerful. They didn't have fancy titles or big bank accounts, but they had something just as valuable: grit and determination. They offered their labor, their resources, even their lives to support the cause of independence. They were the unsung heroes, working tirelessly behind the scenes to make sure the movement kept going.

Now, you might be wondering why these stories are so important. Well, for one thing, they paint a much more complete picture of Pakistan's past. History isn't just about the big names and big events; it's about the everyday people who lived through it. By listening to their stories, we can better understand the challenges they faced, the sacrifices they made, and the hopes they had for their country.

But it goes beyond that. These stories are also a challenge to the way history is often told. We tend to focus on the winners, the heroes, the people in charge. But what about everyone else? By bringing the stories of marginalized groups to the forefront, we're saying that their experiences matter too. We're acknowledging that history isn't a single story, but a collection of many different voices and perspectives.

Think about it this way: Imagine you're putting together a puzzle. You've got all the big pieces in place, but there are still some gaps. You might be able to see the overall picture, but it's not complete. It's the same with history. If we only focus on the dominant narrative, we're missing out on crucial pieces of the puzzle. And when we're missing pieces, we can't fully understand the whole picture.

These hidden stories are like those missing puzzle pieces. They fill in the gaps, add depth and richness, and reveal the true complexity of Pakistan's past. By acknowledging these stories, we're not just making history more accurate; we're making it more inclusive. We're saying that everyone's story deserves to be told, regardless of their background or social status.

So, how do we bring these stories to light? Well, it's not easy. Many of these narratives have been suppressed or ignored for decades. But thanks to the work of historians, researchers, and filmmakers, we're starting to see a shift. People are digging deeper, looking beyond the official records, and giving voice to those who were silenced for so long.

Documentaries are being made, books are being written, and conversations are being started. This is how we change the narrative, one story at a time. By sharing these experiences, we're not just educating ourselves; we're honoring the people who lived through them. We're giving them the recognition they deserve, and we're ensuring that their sacrifices are not forgotten.

It's important to remember that these stories aren't just about the past. They have relevance for the present and the future as well. By understanding the challenges faced by marginalized groups in the past, we can better understand the challenges they face today. We can learn from their resilience, their determination, and their commitment to creating a more just and equitable society.

Their stories can also inspire us to take action. When we see how ordinary people can make a difference, it gives us hope and motivation to do the same. We realize that we don't have to be famous or powerful to create change; we just have to be willing to stand up for what we believe in.

In the end, the stories of marginalized groups in Pakistan's independence movement are a powerful reminder that history is not set in stone. It's a living, breathing thing that is constantly being reinterpreted and rewritten. By bringing these hidden stories to the forefront, we're not just making history more accurate; we're making it more relevant and meaningful for everyone.

So, the next time you hear about Pakistan's independence, don't just think about the famous leaders and political battles. Remember the women who marched in the streets, the religious minorities who fought for their rights, and the everyday people who sacrificed so much for their country. Their stories are the heart and soul of Pakistan's past, and they deserve to be heard.

5

Women's Role

Let's chat about some real trailblazers in Pakistan, women who shattered glass ceilings and fought for gender equality. Their stories aren't just history lessons; they're living inspiration for the ongoing fight against deep-rooted biases.

Fatima Jinnah: The Force Behind the Vision

Imagine being the sister of the founder of a nation. That was Fatima Jinnah. But she wasn't just Muhammad Ali Jinnah's sibling; she was a political powerhouse in her own right. At a time when women were mostly confined to their homes, she stepped into the political arena. She was all about upholding her brother's dream of a democratic Pakistan. But it wasn't just about politics; it was about giving women a voice, a seat at the table, in a world that barely acknowledged them.

Benazir Bhutto: The Trailblazing Prime Minister

Now, let's fast forward a few decades and meet Benazir Bhutto. She didn't just make history; she rewrote it. As the first female Prime Minister of a Muslim-majority country, she shattered so many stereotypes. Think about it – leading a nation in a region where women were often seen as second-class citizens. She proved that women were not just capable but exceptionally talented leaders.

Malala Yousafzai: The Voice of a Generation

Let's bring it to the present day and meet Malala Yousafzai. This young woman faced death threats for speaking up about girls' education. But she didn't back down. She stood up to the Taliban, survived an assassination attempt, and became a global icon for girls' rights. Her story is a reminder that even in the face of extreme adversity, one voice can inspire millions.

The Ripple Effect: Inspiring Change

The impact of these women went far beyond their individual achievements. They lit a fire that spread throughout Pakistan. Fatima Jinnah's involvement in politics encouraged women to step out of their homes and into public life. Benazir Bhutto's leadership proved that women could hold the highest office, inspiring countless others to aim high. Malala Yousafzai's advocacy for girls' education ignited a global movement, pressuring governments to protect the rights of young women.

Think of their stories as seeds planted in the soil of Pakistan. They grew into a network of women's organizations dedicated to fighting for equality. These groups work tirelessly to change unfair laws, raise awareness, and empower women. The seeds that Fatima, Benazir, and Malala planted have grown into a thriving movement.

The Struggle Continues: Women in Politics

Today, Pakistani women are making their mark in politics. It's a slow process, but the progress is undeniable. More women are running for office, winning elections, and shaping policies. Of course, there are still

challenges, but the path these trailblazers paved is making a real difference.

Remember, their courage wasn't just about individual achievements;
it was about challenging a system that held women back. Their stories
are a testament to the power of resilience, determination, and the unwavering belief that every woman deserves an equal chance to succeed.

Lessons Learned: The Fight for Equality

So, what can we learn from these incredible women? First, never underestimate the power of one person to ignite change. Second, resilience
is key; even in the face of adversity, keep fighting for what you believe in.
And finally, remember that progress is rarely a straight line. It's a winding path with setbacks and triumphs, but with determination, anything
is possible.

The fight for gender equality in Pakistan is far from over. But thanks
to the courage and sacrifices of women like Fatima Jinnah, Benazir
Bhutto, and Malala Yousafzai, the future looks a little brighter. They've
shown us that change is possible, one step at a time. Their stories are a
reminder that every single one of us has the power to make a difference,
no matter how big or small.

In the end, it's not just about fighting for equality; it's about creating
a world where every woman can live up to her full potential, where her
dreams are not limited by societal expectations, and where her voice is
heard loud and clear. That's the legacy of these trailblazing women, and
it's a legacy that continues to inspire us all.

Imagine a society where laws are not just words on paper, but
living forces that transform lives. That's the story of women's rights
in Pakistan. It's not just about the laws themselves, but the tireless ac-

tivism that brings them to life. It's a tale of how legal changes and grassroots movements have come together to create real progress in a country where gender equality has often been a struggle.

The Laws That Changed the Game

Let's talk about some game-changing laws. The Protection Against Harassment of Women at the Workplace Act was a huge step forward. It wasn't just about protecting women at work; it was about challenging the idea that women should tolerate harassment in silence. It was a wake-up call to society, saying, "Hey, this isn't okay!"

Then there were the changes to the Penal Code to address honor crimes. These horrific acts of violence against women have been a stain on Pakistani society for far too long. The new laws sent a powerful message: these crimes are not "cultural traditions"; they're illegal and unacceptable.

The Power of Persistent Voices

But laws are just the beginning. It takes passionate people to make those laws a reality. That's where women's rights movements come in. These are groups of women (and men too!) who have been fighting for equality for years, often facing enormous challenges and opposition. They've been lobbying for new laws, pushing for their enforcement, and educating women about their rights.

Imagine a group of women meeting in a small village, sharing their stories of harassment and discrimination, and then learning about a new law that can protect them. That's empowering. It's about giving women the tools they need to fight back against injustice.

More Than Just Words: Real Change

The impact of these laws and activism has been nothing short of revolutionary. Women who were once afraid to speak out are now reporting harassment and getting justice. Families that might have once considered an "honor killing" are now thinking twice because they know it's a serious crime. The very fabric of society is shifting.

Of course, there's still a long way to go. But these changes are not superficial. They're changing minds, one conversation at a time. They're teaching girls that they have the right to an education and a career. They're showing boys that women are not property to be controlled.

The Synergy of Law and Activism

The lesson here is that laws and activism need each other. Laws provide a framework for change, but activism breathes life into those laws. It's like a bicycle – the laws are the wheels, and activism is the pedals. You need both to move forward.

Think of the women's rights movement as a chorus of voices, each one singing a different tune but all working towards the same goal – equality. Some voices are loud and forceful, others are gentle and persuasive, but together, they create a powerful symphony that can't be ignored.

The Journey Continues: A Brighter Future

Pakistan's journey towards gender equality is far from over. There are still challenges ahead. But the progress made so far shows that change is possible. It shows that even in a society steeped in tradition, the voices of those who demand justice can break through.

So, what does the future hold? It's hard to say for sure, but one thing is certain: the women of Pakistan will continue to fight for their rights. They'll continue to challenge the status quo, push for better laws, and educate their communities. And they'll do it with the knowledge that their struggle is not in vain, that their voices are being heard, and that they are making a real difference in the lives of countless women.

The story of women's rights in Pakistan is a testament to the power of the human spirit. It's a story of courage, resilience, and the unwavering belief that every woman deserves to live a life free from discrimination and violence. It's a story that inspires us all to never give up on the fight for justice and equality.

Picture this: Pakistan, a land of vibrant colors, rich history, and immense potential. But within this tapestry, there's a struggle for gender equality, a battle against deeply rooted traditions and stereotypes that hold women back. It's a complex issue, but don't worry, it's not a lost cause.

Think of it like a puzzle. To empower women in Pakistan, we need to find the right pieces and fit them together. Education, leadership, and challenging societal norms are three key pieces that can make a real difference.

Empowering Through Education

Let's start with education. Imagine a young girl in a rural village, eager to learn but facing barriers simply because she's female. By investing in education for girls, we're not just giving them knowledge; we're giving them a voice, a chance to break free from limiting beliefs.

It's like giving them a key to unlock their potential. With education, they can dream bigger, set ambitious goals, and challenge the idea that their place is solely in the home. They become architects of their own futures, and that's a powerful thing.

Leading the Way: Female Role Models

Now, let's talk about leadership. When women take charge, whether in business, politics, or their communities, they shatter stereotypes and inspire others. It's like a domino effect—one woman's success paves the way for countless others to follow.

Imagine a young woman watching a female CEO lead a company or a female politician make impactful decisions. It sends a powerful message: "I can do that too!" These role models break down barriers and show that women are capable of anything.

Challenging the Norms: Changing Minds

But education and leadership alone aren't enough. We need to change hearts and minds. We need to challenge the cultural norms that hold women back. This is where grassroots organizations, public awareness campaigns, and even everyday conversations play a crucial role.

Think of it like untangling a knot. We need to patiently and persistently unravel the threads of discrimination and prejudice that have been woven into the fabric of society for generations. It takes time, effort, and a willingness to have uncomfortable conversations, but it's absolutely essential.

A Multifaceted Approach: It Takes a Village

So, how do we put all these pieces together? It's not a simple answer, but it starts with a multi-pronged approach. We need to:

Invest in girls' education: Provide access to quality education for all girls, regardless of their background.

Empower female leaders: Support and mentor women in various sectors, encouraging them to reach their full potential.

Challenge societal norms: Raise awareness about gender equality through public campaigns, media, and education.

Reform policies: Enact and enforce laws that protect women's rights and promote gender equality.

Engage men and boys: Include men and boys in the conversation about gender equality, emphasizing their role in creating a more equitable society.

It's a team effort, a collaborative endeavor that requires commitment from individuals, communities, and the government. But it's a fight worth fighting.

The Promise of Change

The challenges are real, and the road ahead may be bumpy. But the potential for change is immense. Imagine a Pakistan where every girl has the opportunity to pursue her dreams, where women lead with confidence, and where gender equality is not just an aspiration but a reality.

That's the Pakistan we're working towards. And it's a Pakistan that's within reach. By investing in education, empowering female leaders, and challenging societal norms, we can create a brighter future for all.

The Ripple Effect of Empowerment

The benefits of empowering women are far-reaching. When women thrive, their families thrive, their communities thrive, and the entire nation prospers. It's a win-win situation.

Empowered women are more likely to be educated, healthy, and financially independent. They're more likely to participate in the workforce, contribute to the economy, and make decisions that benefit their families and communities. They're also more likely to raise healthy, educated children who will continue the cycle of progress.

A Call to Action

So, let's roll up our sleeves and get to work. Let's support organizations that are working to empower women. Let's speak out against discrimination and challenge stereotypes. Let's mentor young girls and encourage them to reach for the stars.

The future of Pakistan depends on the empowerment of its women. It's time to break down the barriers that hold them back and create a society where everyone can thrive, regardless of gender.

Hey there, let's have a heart-to-heart about the incredible women leading grassroots movements in Pakistan. You know, those groups of women who are rolling up their sleeves and making real change happen, right in their own communities. It's inspiring stuff, and it's got a lot to teach us about how to make the world a better place for everyone.

Power to the People: The Grassroots Movement

Imagine this: a group of women gathering in a village square, talking about their struggles, their hopes, and their dreams. They might not have fancy degrees or political connections, but they have something even more powerful – a deep understanding of their own communities and a fierce determination to make things better.

That's the essence of a grassroots movement. It's about people taking charge of their own lives, working together to solve problems that have been holding them back for generations. And in Pakistan, women's grassroots movements are leading the charge when it comes to fighting for equality.

Education: A Key to Unlock Potential

One of the most important things these movements do is focus on education. They understand that knowledge is power. When girls are educated, they're not just learning facts and figures; they're learning to think for themselves, to challenge the status quo, and to envision a better future.

Imagine a young girl who's never been to school. She might believe that her only path in life is to get married and have children. But if she has access to education, she learns about different possibilities. She learns about careers she never knew existed, about women who have achieved great things, about her own rights and how to protect them. It opens up a whole new world.

Taking the Lead: Women in Charge

Grassroots movements also focus on empowering women to become leaders. This isn't just about having women in positions of power; it's about changing the very fabric of society. When women are leaders, they bring a different perspective to the table. They prioritize issues like education, healthcare, and childcare – issues that often get overlooked when men are the only ones making decisions.

Think about it: if you want to solve a problem, wouldn't you want the people who are most affected by that problem to have a say in the solution? That's why female leadership is so important. It's about giving women a seat at the table and ensuring their voices are heard.

Breaking Down Barriers: Challenging Norms

But grassroots movements don't stop there. They also challenge harmful societal norms and stereotypes. This is where things get really interesting. Because it's not just about changing laws; it's about changing minds.

These movements work tirelessly to raise awareness about gender equality. They hold workshops, organize community events, and engage in conversations with families, religious leaders, and even government officials. They're not afraid to push back against harmful traditions and beliefs that hold women back.

Making a Difference: One Step at a Time

The impact of these movements is undeniable. In Pakistan, women's grassroots groups have made significant strides in improving access to education and healthcare. They've fought against child marriage, domestic violence, and discrimination. They've created safe spaces for women to share their stories and find support.

But it's not just about the tangible results; it's about the ripple effect. When one woman is empowered, it inspires others. It creates a sense of hope and possibility. It shows that change is not only possible but happening right now.

The Way Forward: A Collective Effort

The fight for gender equality in Pakistan is far from over. There are still many challenges ahead. But the women leading these grassroots movements are not giving up. They're determined to create a better future for themselves, their families, and their communities.

And they're not alone. There are countless organizations, both local and international, that are supporting their efforts. Governments are starting to recognize the importance of investing in women's empowerment. And most importantly, there's a growing awareness among the Pakistani people that gender equality is not just a women's issue; it's an issue that affects everyone.

So, what can we do to support these incredible women? We can donate to organizations that are working on the ground. We can amplify their voices on social media. We can educate ourselves about the challenges women face in Pakistan and around the world. And we can challenge our own biases and assumptions.

Remember, change doesn't happen overnight. It's a slow and steady process, but it's a process that's worth fighting for. And with the determination and resilience of Pakistan's grassroots women's movements, the future looks brighter than ever.

6

Urbanization Dynamics

The Great Pakistani Shuffle: Cities, Dreams, and the Price of Progress

Alright, folks, gather round for a story about Pakistan. Not the usual headlines of politics and cricket, but a tale of dreams, hard graft, and the relentless pull of city lights. It's about a phenomenon we call rural-to-urban migration. In plain terms, it's the story of millions of folks leaving their villages behind and heading for the big cities.

Why the Big Move? The Dream of a Better Life

Now, you might wonder, why would anyone trade the peace and quiet of the countryside for the hustle and bustle of the city? Well, there's more to it than meets the eye.

First and foremost, it's about money. The cities, with their shiny offices and bustling markets, promise jobs and wages that are simply unheard of back in the village. A farmer struggling to make ends meet might become a taxi driver or a construction worker in the city, earning enough to send money back home and support his family.

Then, there's the education. The cities have the best schools and colleges. Parents dream of their children becoming doctors, engineers, or even professors. They see education as a ladder out of poverty and a way to a brighter future.

But it's not just about material things. It's also about status. City life, with its modern amenities and cosmopolitan culture, is seen as a step up the social ladder. It's about having a better house, nicer clothes, and the ability to provide a better life for your family.

The City of Dreams: Reality Bites

However, the reality of city life often turns out to be different from the dream. The streets paved with gold often turn out to be crowded, dusty, and noisy. Finding a decent place to live is a nightmare. Rents are sky-high, and many migrants end up crammed into slums or informal settlements, far from the idealized city of their dreams.

Then, there's the culture shock. The city, with its different customs, language, and social norms, can be overwhelming. Imagine a simple villager used to the slower pace of rural life suddenly thrown into the chaos of a big city. It's like landing on a different planet.

Making friends and building a support network can be difficult. The anonymity of city life can be isolating, leaving many migrants feeling lonely and homesick.

The Silver Lining: Progress and Opportunity

Despite these challenges, the move to the city is not without its rewards. Migrants often find better-paying jobs, access to healthcare and education, and a chance to improve their standard of living. Their children have the opportunity to attend better schools and pursue higher education.

Even though the transition is tough, many migrants eventually adapt to city life. They learn the ropes, make friends, and find their footing in the urban jungle. They become part of the city's vibrant fabric, contributing to its growth and development.

The Bigger Picture: A Changing Nation

Rural-to-urban migration is not just about individual lives; it's a force that's reshaping the entire nation. Cities are growing at an unprecedented rate, straining infrastructure and resources. But they're also becoming hubs of innovation, entrepreneurship, and creativity.

The migrants, with their energy, ambition, and diverse skills, are playing a crucial role in this transformation. They're the backbone of the urban economy, working in factories, construction sites, and service industries. They're starting businesses, driving innovation, and enriching the city's cultural landscape.

Challenges Ahead: A Balancing Act

The challenges are immense. Cities need to find ways to accommodate the growing influx of migrants, provide them with decent housing, and integrate them into the urban fabric. They need to create jobs, improve infrastructure, and address the social and cultural tensions that arise from rapid urbanization.

The government, civil society organizations, and the private sector all have a role to play in this. It's about creating a more inclusive and equitable urban environment, where everyone has a chance to succeed, regardless of their background.

In Conclusion: A Story of Hope and Resilience

The story of rural-to-urban migration in Pakistan is a complex one, full of contradictions and paradoxes. It's a story of dreams and disappointments, of hope and hardship, of loss and gain.

But above all, it's a story of human resilience, adaptability, and the relentless pursuit of a better life. It's a testament to the human spirit, which refuses to be defeated by adversity and keeps striving for a brighter future.

The journey is far from over. The challenges are real, and the road ahead is uncertain. But one thing is clear: rural-to-urban migration is a force that's here to stay, and it's reshaping Pakistan in profound ways.

Building Pakistan's Cities: A Balancing Act Between Past and Present

Picture this: Pakistan's cities, like bustling Karachi or historic Lahore, are like a living, breathing time capsule. They carry the echoes of colonial-era city planning, while simultaneously grappling with the chaotic energy of rapid urbanization. It's a captivating story of how the past and present collide, shaping the very fabric of our urban landscapes.

Colonial Echoes in Modern Pakistan

Let's rewind to the colonial era, when the British laid the foundation for many of Pakistan's major cities. Back then, cities were smaller, life was slower, and these urban plans worked pretty well. Think of tree-lined avenues, neat grids, and spacious bungalows.

Fast forward to today, and these cities have exploded in size. It's like trying to squeeze into your childhood clothes after a growth spurt. The colonial blueprint, designed for a quieter time, is now bursting at the seams. The result? Traffic jams that could rival a snail race, public transport systems packed like sardine cans, and waste management problems that stink to high heaven.

Growing Pains: The Challenge of Sustainability

And it's not just about creaky infrastructure. The way we build cities today has a huge impact on the environment. We're talking about pollution, resource depletion, and climate change. If we don't get smart about our urban planning, we risk creating cities that are not only uncomfortable but unsustainable.

Karachi, for instance, is a city of stark contrasts. On one hand, it's a buzzing metropolis with a booming economy. On the other hand, it's grappling with severe water shortages, traffic congestion, and pollution that could choke a horse. These are not just growing pains, they're warning signs that we need to change our approach.

Lessons from History: Building Smarter Cities

The good news is, we don't have to reinvent the wheel. We can learn from the past, even as we embrace the future. The colonial-era city plans, with their emphasis on open spaces, green areas, and walkable neighborhoods, offer valuable lessons in sustainable design.

At the same time, we need to adopt modern solutions like smart technology, renewable energy, and efficient public transport systems. We need to think long-term, invest in sustainable infrastructure, and create cities that are not just livable but also environmentally friendly.

Lahore: A City Caught in Time

Lahore, the cultural heart of Pakistan, is a perfect example of this balancing act. Its historic walled city, with its narrow lanes, bustling markets, and grand Mughal architecture, is a treasure trove of cultural heritage.

But as the city expands beyond the old walls, it faces the same challenges as other rapidly growing cities. Traffic congestion, inadequate public transport, and haphazard development are threatening to erode its charm and character.

The challenge for Lahore, as for other Pakistani cities, is to find a way to preserve its heritage while embracing the future. It's about finding a balance between tradition and modernity, between preservation and progress.

The Way Forward: A Holistic Approach

The key lies in taking a holistic approach to urban planning. It's not just about building roads and bridges; it's about creating communities where people can live, work, and play. It's about designing cities that are inclusive, equitable, and sustainable.

This means involving all stakeholders, from government officials and urban planners to community leaders and ordinary citizens. It means listening to different voices, considering different perspectives, and working together to create a shared vision for the future.

It also means investing in education and awareness-raising. We need to teach our children about the importance of sustainability and responsible urban planning. We need to empower citizens to become active participants in shaping their cities.

The Future is Urban: Building a Better Pakistan

The future of Pakistan is undeniably urban. More and more people are moving to cities in search of a better life. The challenge is to ensure that our cities are not just engines of economic growth, but also vibrant, livable, and sustainable communities.

This is not just a challenge for urban planners and policymakers. It's a challenge for all of us. We all have a stake in creating cities that we can be proud of, cities that reflect our values, our culture, and our aspirations.

By learning from the past, embracing the present, and planning for the future, we can build a better Pakistan, one city at a time.

Weaving the Urban Tapestry: Building Community in Pakistan's Melting Pots

Picture this: Karachi's bustling bazaars, a whirlwind of colors, sounds, and aromas. Or Lahore's historic streets, where centuries-old architecture meets modern cafes and bustling markets. These cities are microcosms of Pakistan's diverse cultural landscape, places where people from all walks of life come together to live, work, and play.

But creating a sense of community in such diverse urban environments is no easy feat. It's like trying to make a delicious biryani with a hundred different spices. Each ingredient brings its own unique flavor, and if not blended carefully, the dish can become a chaotic mess.

More than Just Diversity: The Importance of Inclusion

Diversity is a beautiful thing, but it's not enough. Imagine a classroom where every student speaks a different language. Without a common tongue, they wouldn't be able to understand each other, let alone learn together.

The same goes for cities. Diversity alone doesn't automatically lead to harmony. We need something more: inclusion. This means creating spaces where everyone feels welcome, respected, and valued, regardless of their background. It means ensuring that everyone has a voice, and that their voice is heard.

Participatory Governance: The Key to Social Cohesion

So, how do we achieve this? One crucial ingredient is participatory governance. It's like having a town hall meeting where everyone gets to share their ideas and concerns. It's about giving people a seat at the table and involving them in the decision-making process.

Take a community in Karachi, for instance. They might be facing issues like lack of clean water, poor sanitation, or inadequate infrastructure. If the residents are simply told what to do by the government, they might feel resentful and disconnected.

But if they're actively involved in finding solutions, they become invested in the outcome. They take ownership of the problems and work together to find solutions. This not only builds trust and cooperation, but it also leads to more effective and sustainable solutions.

Case Studies: The Power of Community Engagement

Across Pakistan, there are inspiring examples of how participatory governance is making a real difference. In Lahore, residents of a low-income neighborhood came together to transform a neglected park into a vibrant community space. They organized clean-up drives, planted trees, and installed playground equipment. The park became a hub for social interaction, where people from different backgrounds could come together and build relationships.

In Karachi, a group of women started a community kitchen to provide meals for the homeless and elderly. They also organized workshops on health, hygiene, and financial literacy, empowering women and building a sense of community ownership.

These are just a few examples of how ordinary citizens are taking the initiative to make their cities better. By working together, they're not only improving their own lives, but they're also strengthening the social fabric of their communities.

The Role of Education: Shaping Inclusive Citizens

Education plays a crucial role in this process. Schools are not just places to learn facts and figures; they're also where children learn about citizenship, democracy, and the importance of social responsibility.

Imagine a classroom where students from different backgrounds learn together, share their experiences, and challenge each other's perspectives. This kind of inclusive education helps break down stereotypes, fosters empathy, and prepares young people to become active and engaged citizens.

Building a Brighter Future: The Road Ahead

The road to social cohesion is not without its challenges. There are deep-seated prejudices, economic disparities, and political tensions that need to be addressed. But by focusing on inclusivity, diversity, and participatory governance, we can create a society where everyone feels valued and has a stake in the future.

Pakistan's cities are like a vibrant mosaic, each piece representing a different culture, language, and religion. By working together, we can create a beautiful picture, a society where diversity is celebrated, inclusion is a way of life, and everyone has the opportunity to thrive.

The Tale of Two Pakistans: Cities, Villages, and the Dance of Dependence

Ever heard the saying, "You scratch my back, I'll scratch yours"? That's the gist of how Pakistan's cities and villages get along. It's like a big, messy family dinner, where everyone brings something different to the table, but sometimes, not everyone gets an equal share of the pie.

The City Slickers and the Country Folks: A Love-Hate Relationship

Let's break it down. The big cities, like Karachi and Lahore, are like the cool kids at school. They've got the fancy clothes (read: infrastructure), the best toys (hospitals, universities), and all the job opportunities.

But guess what? They're not as self-sufficient as they think. They need the village folks, the farmers and producers, to feed them. Without the fresh fruits, vegetables, and grains that come from the rural areas, those city markets would be pretty empty.

And what about the villagers? Well, they need the cities too. They rely on urban markets to sell their produce and get a fair price. They need the city hospitals for healthcare, the universities for education, and the factories for jobs when farming isn't enough.

It's a classic case of interdependence. But here's the catch: this relationship isn't always fair and square.

The Uneven Playing Field: Who Gets the Bigger Slice?

While the cities and villages need each other, there's a huge difference in their standard of living. The cities are hogging most of the resources. They have better roads, schools, hospitals, and job opportunities. It's like the older sibling who always gets the bigger slice of cake.

Meanwhile, the villages are often left behind, struggling with poor infrastructure, limited access to healthcare and education, and a lack of jobs. It's like the younger sibling who's always left with the crumbs.

This imbalance isn't just unfair; it's also a recipe for trouble. It breeds resentment, fuels social unrest, and holds back the entire country's progress.

The Need for Balance: A Fair Share for All

So, what's the solution? We need to level the playing field. We need to make sure that both urban and rural areas get their fair share of the pie.

This means investing in rural infrastructure, improving access to healthcare and education, and creating job opportunities in the countryside. It means supporting farmers and producers so they can get a fair price for their goods.

But it's not just about throwing money at the problem. It's about smart planning and sustainable development. It's about creating policies that benefit both urban and rural communities, that foster collaboration and mutual respect.

A Vision for the Future: Cities and Villages Thriving Together

Imagine a Pakistan where every child, whether they live in a bustling city or a quiet village, has access to quality education and healthcare.

Imagine a Pakistan where farmers can earn a decent living from their hard work, and where young people don't have to leave their homes in search of jobs.

Imagine a Pakistan where cities and villages are not rivals, but partners in progress, where the vibrancy of urban life complements the tranquility of rural living.

This might sound like a distant dream, but it's a dream worth striving for. By working together, by recognizing our interdependence, and by investing in equitable development, we can create a Pakistan where everyone has the opportunity to thrive.

The Bottom Line: It's Time for a Change

The tale of two Pakistans is a story of challenges, but it's also a story of hope. We have the potential to transform our country, to bridge the gap between urban and rural areas, and to create a society that's truly inclusive and equitable.

But it's not going to be easy. It will require bold leadership, innovative thinking, and a willingness to challenge the status quo. It will require us to rethink our priorities and invest in the future of all our citizens, not just a privileged few.

It's a journey that will take time, effort, and commitment. But the rewards will be worth it. A Pakistan where cities and villages thrive together is a Pakistan that's stronger, more resilient, and more prosperous. It's a Pakistan that we can all be proud to call home.

7

Political Revolution

Alright, let's dive into the fascinating world of Pakistan's grassroots movements. Now, this isn't your everyday political story. It's more like a whisper network of changemakers, quietly but steadily shifting the power dynamics in the country.

Imagine a tapestry woven with threads of social justice, environmental concerns, and a yearning for a government that actually listens to its people. That's what grassroots movements are about in Pakistan. They're not just protests or campaigns; they're a reflection of a society finding its voice and demanding change.

So, how do these movements work? They're like chameleons, adapting to the environment they're in. In small villages, you'll see traditional community organizing at its best. Elders gather under trees, women share stories over chai, and young people dream of a brighter future. This is where the roots of change begin to sprout.

Then there's the digital dimension, where hashtags and viral videos can spread a message faster than wildfire. These movements aren't afraid to embrace technology to amplify their voices and reach a wider audience. They're tweeting, posting, and sharing stories that mainstream media often overlooks.

Think of it like a two-pronged attack. On the ground, they're building trust and solidarity within communities. Online, they're creating a digital echo chamber that's hard to ignore. This combination is powerful because it forces those in power to take notice.

Now, let's talk about what these movements are fighting for. It's not just about politics; it's about everyday life. They're fighting for clean water, education for girls, and protection for marginalized communities. They're raising their voices against corruption, injustice, and the exploitation of natural resources.

And you know what's truly inspiring? These movements are led by ordinary people. They're not career politicians or wealthy elites; they're teachers, farmers, students, and activists who are passionate about making a difference. They're the unsung heroes of Pakistan's democracy.

Now, let's get a little more specific. Remember the parallel theatre movement? It's a fantastic example of how grassroots activism can take unexpected forms. This movement uses theatre to engage young people, especially in rural areas, sparking conversations about social issues and encouraging them to take action. It's art with a purpose, and it's incredibly effective.

Then there's the women's movement, which has been a force to be reckoned with since the 1980s. Women from all walks of life have come together to fight for their rights, challenge discriminatory laws, and demand a seat at the table. Their courage and determination have inspired countless others to join the fight for equality.

But it's not just about social justice. Environmental issues are also high on the agenda. Grassroots movements are leading the charge to protect Pakistan's natural beauty, from the towering mountains to the fertile plains. They're planting trees, cleaning up rivers, and fighting against pollution. They understand that a healthy environment is essential for a healthy society.

Of course, it's not an easy road. These movements face challenges like limited resources, political pressure, and even threats to their safety. But they persevere because they believe in a better Pakistan, a country where everyone has a voice and a chance to thrive.

So, what's the impact of all this grassroots activism? It's slowly but surely changing the political landscape. These movements are injecting fresh ideas, raising critical questions, and demanding accountability from those in power. They're pushing for policies that reflect the needs and aspirations of ordinary people.

They're also creating a sense of hope and empowerment. When people see that their voices can make a difference, they're more likely to get involved and hold their leaders accountable. This is how democracy thrives, from the ground up.

In the end, grassroots movements in Pakistan are a testament to the resilience and creativity of the human spirit. They remind us that change is possible, even in the face of overwhelming odds. They give us hope that a more just, equitable, and sustainable future is within reach.

So, the next time you hear about a protest, a campaign, or a group of people fighting for their rights in Pakistan, remember that it's not just about politics. It's about people power, and it's a force that's transforming the nation one step at a time.

Let's have a real chat about Pakistan's history, not the sugarcoated version you might hear on the news or read in textbooks. Instead, let's dig deeper into the stories that often get swept under the rug – the stories of the everyday people, the different regions, and the women who have shaped the country in ways we don't always hear about.

The official story of Pakistan often focuses on a unified vision, like everyone agreed on what it meant to be Pakistani from the start. But the reality is far more colorful and complex. If you listen to the stories of marginalized groups, regional movements, and women, you get a completely different picture – one that's filled with challenges, resistance, and a constant struggle for power.

Take the Left in Pakistan, for example. They weren't just a bunch of rebels; they had a whole different idea of what the country should look like, one that clashed with the government's vision. And they weren't alone. Throughout history, countless groups and individuals have found themselves at odds with the dominant narrative, offering their own interpretations of Pakistan's identity and political scene.

These alternative viewpoints do more than just criticize the mainstream narrative; they challenge us to rethink everything we thought we knew about Pakistan. They show us that the story isn't just about a unified nation, but about a diverse group of people with different identities, struggles, and dreams.

One of the most powerful examples of this is the way women's experiences have often been ignored or minimized in traditional histories. But when you listen to the stories of women throughout Pakistan's history, you see a completely different picture. You see women not just as victims, but as strong, resilient individuals fighting against inequality and shaping the country in their own way.

And it's not just women. Regional movements, too, offer a different perspective on what it means to be Pakistani. They remind us that the country isn't just one big, homogenous mass but a collection of diverse regions, each with its own unique identity and struggles.

Think about the textbooks you might have read in school. They often present a very simplistic view of history, glossing over the economic motives and the voices of marginalized groups. But when you dig deeper, you find a much richer tapestry of stories – stories of economic struggles, power struggles, and resistance movements that have shaped Pakistan in profound ways.

Take the partition of India and Pakistan, for example. The violence and displacement that occurred during this time were traumatic events that have had a lasting impact on the country. Yet, these experiences are often glossed over in official histories, leaving a gap in our understanding of Pakistan's identity.

But when we delve into these alternative narratives, we start to see the partition not just as a historical event, but as a deep wound that continues to shape the nation. We see how it has created tensions and divisions that persist to this day, shaping how people define themselves as Pakistani.

By listening to these different voices and perspectives, we can start to build a more complete picture of Pakistan's history. We can understand how different groups have shaped and been shaped by the country's political landscape. We can see the complexity of identities, the struggles for power, and the constant push and pull between different forces.

This isn't just about rewriting history; it's about understanding who we are as a nation. It's about recognizing the diversity of our experiences and the complexity of our struggles. It's about acknowledging the voices that have been silenced or marginalized and giving them a place in our national story.

And it's not just about the past. These alternative narratives also have a lot to teach us about the present. By understanding the struggles of marginalized groups, regional movements, and women, we can gain valuable insights into the challenges facing Pakistan today. We can see how these historical experiences continue to shape our society and how they can inform our efforts to build a more just and equitable future.

So, the next time you hear someone talking about Pakistan's history, don't just accept the official version at face value. Ask questions. Dig deeper. Seek out the voices that are often left out of the conversation. You might be surprised at what you find. You might discover a history that's richer, more complex, and more relevant to our lives today than you ever imagined.

This is the essence of inclusive historiography. It's about acknowledging that there's no single, definitive version of history. It's about recognizing that everyone's experiences and perspectives matter, and that our understanding of the past is always evolving. It's about embracing the complexity of our history and using it to build a better future.

Let's not forget that the story of Pakistan is not just about the powerful and privileged. It's about the everyday people, the marginalized groups, the regional movements, and the women who have struggled, resisted, and persevered in the face of adversity. Their stories matter, and they deserve to be heard.

Alright folks, let's have a heart-to-heart about the young guns shaking things up in Pakistan. We're not just talking about kids getting involved in politics; we're talking about a full-blown youthquake that's transforming the nation's entire social and political landscape.

Picture this: a wave of young people, full of energy and passion, taking to the streets, social media, and even the parliament. They're not just making noise; they're leading the charge for change, pushing for reforms, and holding the old guard accountable.

One of the most striking examples of this youthquake is the rise of the Pakistan Tehreek-e-Insaf (PTI) party. This party didn't just come out of nowhere; it was fueled by the passion and dedication of young voters who were fed up with the old ways of doing things. They wanted a new kind of politics, one that addressed their concerns and reflected their values. And they got it. The PTI's rise to power sent shockwaves through the political establishment, forcing other parties to sit up and take notice of the youth vote.

But it's not just about who's in charge; it's about the issues that matter to young people. Take education, for example. Malala Yousafzai, the young Nobel Peace Prize laureate, has become a global icon for girls' education. Through her Malala Fund, she's not only raising awareness about the importance of education but also pushing for real policy changes that can make a difference in the lives of millions of girls around the world.

And it's not just big names like Malala. All across Pakistan, young people are taking the lead in education advocacy, organizing campaigns, lobbying politicians, and creating innovative solutions to educational challenges. They're showing us that education isn't just a right; it's a powerful tool for social change.

Now, let's talk about climate change. You might think this is an issue that only concerns scientists and policymakers, but you'd be wrong. Young people in Pakistan are leading the charge for climate action, organizing protests, demanding sustainable policies, and holding leaders accountable for their inaction.

Campaigns like "Fridays for Future" have become a global phenomenon, with young people all over the world demanding action on climate change. In Pakistan, this movement has taken on a unique flavor, reflecting the specific environmental challenges facing the country. From air pollution to water scarcity, young activists are raising their voices and demanding that their government take immediate and meaningful action to protect their future.

What's so amazing about all of this is that it's not just happening in one city or one region. It's a nationwide phenomenon. Whether you're in the bustling cities of Punjab or the remote villages of Balochistan, you'll find young people who are politically aware, engaged, and determined to make a difference.

Social media has played a huge role in this. It's given young people a platform to express their views, connect with each other, and organize movements for change. They're not just talking about politics; they're actively participating in it, shaping the national conversation and pushing for reforms that reflect their values.

Studies have shown that a large number of young Pakistanis are actively engaged in political discourse online. They're sharing news, debating issues, and mobilizing support for causes they care about. This digital activism has had a real impact, influencing policy decisions and holding leaders accountable.

But it's not just about online activism. Young people are also taking to the streets, organizing protests, and demanding to be heard. They're showing us that they're not content to sit on the sidelines and watch; they want to be part of the decision-making process.

This growing political awareness among the youth is a sign of hope for Pakistan. It shows that there's a new generation of leaders emerging, one that's more inclusive, more progressive, and more determined to create a better future for their country.

So, what does all this mean for the future of Pakistan? Well, it means that the old ways of doing things are being challenged. It means that the traditional political parties can no longer ignore the concerns of young people. It means that the voices of the marginalized are being amplified. And it means that Pakistan is on the cusp of a new era, one that's being shaped by the energy, passion, and determination of its youth.

The young people of Pakistan are not just the leaders of tomorrow; they're the leaders of today. They're the ones who are pushing for change, demanding accountability, and shaping the future of their country. And that's something worth celebrating.

Hey there, let's dive into the wild world of Pakistani politics! It's a bit of a rollercoaster, with political parties facing a ton of challenges that make it tough for them to be effective and win elections. Think of it like a team sport where everyone's got their own ideas about how to play, the coach isn't really calling the shots, and they keep changing players mid-game. Chaos, right?

One of the biggest headaches is internal factionalism. Imagine a team where different players are constantly bickering, each trying to be the star player. That's what's happening inside many Pakistani political parties. It creates a mess where it's hard to make decisions, the party's message gets all muddled, and voters get confused about what they stand for.

And speaking of voters, another big issue is that parties often have outdated playbooks. They're not keeping up with what people care about. It's like using a 1990s game plan in a modern-day match – it just doesn't work. So, they need to get with the times and figure out what issues resonate with voters today.

Then there's the whole coalition thing. Think of it like trying to form a team from a bunch of different sports. You've got football players, basketball players, and maybe even a cricket player thrown in for good measure. Getting everyone to play together and agree on a common goal is tough, and it's the same in politics. Parties need to build strong coalitions, but it's a real challenge when everyone has different priorities.

So, what's the solution to all this mess? Well, it's not easy, but there are some things parties can do to get their act together.

First, they need to work on internal unity. Instead of fighting each other, they need to find common ground and create a clear, unified message that everyone can get behind. This might mean giving all party members a real voice in decision-making, not just the top dogs. It's like having a team meeting where everyone gets to share their ideas, not just the coach.

Next, they need to update their game plan. That means using data and research to figure out what issues matter most to voters. It's like scouting the opposing team so you can develop strategies that are actually effective. Parties need to be nimble and adaptable, ready to change their tactics based on what's happening on the ground.

Finally, they need to get better at building coalitions. This means finding common goals with other parties and focusing on those, rather than just trying to grab power. It's like forming a league where different teams can work together for the good of the sport.

It's not going to be easy, but by following these steps, Pakistani political parties can overcome their organizational challenges and become more effective. This will not only benefit the parties themselves but also the entire country. After all, a healthy and functioning democracy relies on strong political parties that can represent the interests of the people and create effective policies.

And let's be real, the stakes are high. Pakistan is facing a host of challenges, from economic instability to climate change to social inequality. To tackle these issues, the country needs political parties that are united, adaptable, and responsive to the needs of the people.

So, let's hope that Pakistani political parties are up to the task. They have the potential to be powerful forces for good, but they need to get their house in order first. With the right strategies and a commitment to unity, they can overcome their challenges and build a brighter future for Pakistan.

8

Economic Paradigms

Picture this: The Indus River valley, a vast expanse of fertile land where ancient farmers toiled under the scorching sun, coaxing life from the earth. It's a scene that has played out for centuries, shaping the very fabric of Pakistan's agrarian heart. But this tale of tradition and toil is more than just a historical footnote – it's a living legacy that continues to shape Pakistan's economy and society today.

Let's take a stroll through time, shall we? Imagine the ancient farmers, their hands calloused and weathered from generations of working the land. They learned from their ancestors, passing down knowledge of crops, seasons, and the delicate balance of nature. These traditional farming practices, honed over centuries, became the backbone of Pakistan's agrarian economy.

But Pakistan's agricultural story is not a simple one. It's a complex tapestry woven with threads of history, culture, and socio-economic dynamics. Imagine a land where grand feudal estates coexist with small, individually owned plots, and where communal lands are shared by entire villages. These diverse land ownership patterns have shaped not only agricultural productivity but also the very fabric of social relationships in rural Pakistan.

Now, let's fast-forward to the era of the mighty Mughals. Picture grand irrigation systems crisscrossing the landscape, carrying life-giving water to thirsty fields. These engineering marvels, a testament to human ingenuity, revolutionized agriculture in the region. Fast forward again to the present day, and we see modern tractors and combine harvesters working alongside traditional tools like wooden plows and bullock carts. This juxtaposition of old and new is a testament to the resilience and adaptability of Pakistani farmers.

So, what does all of this mean for Pakistan today? Well, it's a mixed bag, really. On the one hand, traditional farming practices and land ownership patterns provide a sense of stability and continuity. They represent a deep connection to the land and a way of life that has sustained generations. On the other hand, these same factors can also hinder progress and perpetuate inequality. Feudal structures, for example, can concentrate power and resources in the hands of a few, leaving small farmers struggling to make ends meet.

But amidst these challenges, there are also signs of hope. Pakistan's agricultural sector is undergoing a transformation, driven by new technologies, innovative farming practices, and a growing awareness of the importance of sustainable agriculture. This transformation is not without its challenges, but it represents a promising step towards a more equitable and prosperous future for Pakistan's farmers.

Let's dive deeper into some of these issues. Take, for instance, the traditional practice of crop rotation. For centuries, farmers have understood the importance of rotating crops to maintain soil fertility and prevent pest outbreaks. This practice is not only environmentally sustainable but also economically sound. However, with the advent of modern fertilizers and pesticides, some farmers have abandoned crop rotation in favor of monoculture farming, which can lead to soil degradation and increased vulnerability to pests and diseases.

Another key issue is water management. Pakistan is a water-stressed country, and agriculture accounts for the vast majority of water usage. Traditional irrigation systems, while efficient in their own right, can be wasteful and contribute to water scarcity. Modern drip irrigation systems, on the other hand, deliver water directly to the roots of plants, minimizing wastage and maximizing yields. But these systems can be expensive, making them inaccessible to many small farmers.

The issue of land ownership is perhaps the most complex and contentious. Feudal structures, inherited from the colonial era, continue to hold sway in many parts of Pakistan. These structures not only concentrate wealth and power in the hands of a few but also perpetuate social hierarchies and limit opportunities for small farmers. Land reforms, aimed at redistributing land and empowering small farmers, have been attempted in the past but have met with limited success due to political resistance and lack of implementation.

But despite these challenges, there is reason for optimism. A new generation of Pakistani farmers is emerging, armed with education, technology, and a passion for sustainable agriculture. They are experimenting with new crops, adopting innovative farming practices, and organizing themselves into cooperatives to gain bargaining power and access to markets. This new generation represents the future of Pakistan's agricultural sector.

The government is also playing a role in supporting agricultural development. Initiatives such as the Prime Minister's Agriculture Emergency Program aim to boost agricultural productivity, improve water management, and provide financial assistance to small farmers. While these initiatives are still in their early stages, they represent a significant step towards a more sustainable and equitable agricultural sector.

So, what does the future hold for Pakistan's agrarian heart? It's diffi-cult to say for sure, but one thing is clear: the traditional farming prac-tices, complex land ownership patterns, and agricultural innovations that have shaped Pakistan's agricultural landscape for centuries will con-tinue to play a vital role in the years to come. Whether these factors will hinder or help progress remains to be seen. But one thing is certain: the story of Pakistan's agrarian heart is far from over. It is a story of re-silience, adaptability, and the enduring spirit of the Pakistani farmer.

As we look to the future, it is important to remember the lessons of the past. Traditional farming practices, while valuable, must be adapted to meet the challenges of a changing world. Land ownership patterns must be reformed to ensure greater equity and opportunity for all farm-ers. And agricultural innovations must be embraced to boost produc-tivity and sustainability.

The path ahead may be uncertain, but one thing is clear: the future of Pakistan's agrarian heart is intertwined with the fate of its farmers. By empowering farmers, investing in agriculture, and embracing sustain-able practices, Pakistan can build a brighter future for its rural commu-nities and ensure the continued prosperity of its agrarian heart.

The story of Pakistan's agrarian heart is a testament to the enduring spirit of the Pakistani farmer. It is a story of resilience, adaptability, and the unwavering determination to overcome challenges. As we look to the future, we must remember the lessons of the past and embrace the opportunities of the present. By working together, we can build a more sustainable, equitable, and prosperous future for Pakistan's agrar-ian heart.

Picture this: Pakistan, a land historically tied to its agrarian roots, is undergoing a dramatic makeover. We're not talking about a fashion show here, but rather a seismic shift in its economy from farming to factories. This change is as dramatic as swapping a dusty field for a bustling city street.

Let's start with the stars of this new show: industries like textiles and cement. They've become the headliners, drawing in both local and foreign investors, turning cities like Karachi and Lahore into manufacturing powerhouses. Think of it as a Broadway production, with these industries taking center stage and the cities providing the backdrop.

But behind the glitz and glamour of this economic transformation lies a more complex story. The rise of these industries has brought about a whole new cast of characters: the workers. These folks, from all walks of life, are flocking to the cities in search of jobs and a better life. It's like a grand migration, with people leaving behind their rural homes for the promise of a brighter future.

But this isn't always a happily ever after scenario. While the new jobs offer opportunities for upward mobility, they also bring challenges. Imagine workers facing long hours, unsafe conditions, and low wages. It's a far cry from the idyllic life they may have envisioned.

And that's not all. The rapid influx of people into the cities is putting a strain on resources and infrastructure. It's like trying to squeeze a large crowd into a small theater – things are bound to get cramped and uncomfortable.

So, what does all of this mean for Pakistan? Well, it's a mixed bag. On the one hand, the industrialization process is driving economic growth and creating new jobs. It's like a rising tide that lifts all boats, at least in theory. On the other hand, it's also creating new inequalities and exacerbating existing ones. The rich are getting richer, while the poor are struggling to keep up.

But let's not get too bogged down in the doom and gloom. There are also positive aspects to this story. The rise of industries is leading to the development of new skills and technologies. It's like a school for the workforce, where people are learning new trades and adapting to the changing demands of the economy.

Moreover, the government is taking steps to address the challenges associated with industrialization. They're investing in infrastructure, promoting worker rights, and trying to create a more equitable playing field for all. It's like a referee stepping in to ensure fair play in a game that's gotten a bit out of hand.

So, what does the future hold for Pakistan's economy? Well, that's the million-dollar question, isn't it? The truth is, no one can say for sure. But one thing is certain: the transition from an agrarian to an industrial economy is a complex and multifaceted process. It's a story of opportunities and challenges, of progress and setbacks.

But perhaps the most important lesson we can learn from this story is that economic development is not just about numbers and statistics. It's about people. It's about the workers who toil in factories, the farmers who still work the land, and the families who are striving for a better life.

Ultimately, the success of Pakistan's economic transformation will depend on its ability to create an environment where everyone has the opportunity to thrive. This means investing in education, healthcare, and infrastructure. It means protecting worker rights and ensuring that the benefits of economic growth are shared equitably.

The road ahead may be long and winding, but with careful planning, sound policies, and a commitment to social justice, Pakistan can navigate the challenges of industrialization and build a brighter future for all its citizens.

You know, Pakistan's got this whole informal sector thing going on, like street vendors in Karachi, small shops in Lahore – that kind of stuff. It's a big deal, giving tons of people jobs and pumping a surprising amount of money into the economy. But there's a catch – it's mostly unregulated.

The Wild West of the Economy

Imagine a business world without rules. That's pretty much the informal sector. It's unpredictable, to say the least. One day you're raking in cash, the next, who knows? Plus, most of these folks can't get loans or anything from banks, which makes it super hard to grow.

The Case for "Formalization"

So, what's the fix? "Formalization." Basically, bringing these informal businesses into the official fold. It's like inviting them to the grown-up table of the economy.

Why Formalization Matters

This isn't just about paperwork. Formalization gives these businesses a safety net – rules and regulations that protect them and their workers. And when they're official, banks are more likely to lend them money, which means they can actually invest in their business and expand.

Stories from the Streets

Think of it this way: A woman in Rawalpindi makes beautiful handicrafts, but she sells them on the street corner. With formalization, she could get a small shop, maybe even hire some help. Or a guy in Karachi who fixes bikes out of his garage. With a loan, he could open a proper repair shop and offer more services.

Incentives Make it Happen

Of course, change isn't easy. But the government can sweeten the deal. Imagine tax breaks for those who go legit, or special loans for small businesses. It's like a "welcome to the club" gift basket.

More than Just Money

Formalization isn't just good for business owners, it's good for the whole country. Think about it: more taxes paid, more jobs created, and a more stable economy. It's a win-win.

The Gender Factor

And let's not forget – women make up a huge part of this informal workforce. They're often doing amazing things, but they face extra hurdles because of, well, just being women. Formalization can help level the playing field, giving them the recognition and opportunities they deserve.

Data Doesn't Lie

I know this might sound like a bunch of theories, but the numbers back it up. Studies have shown that when countries make formalization easier, more businesses join the formal sector, and the economy as a whole gets stronger.

What's Stopping Us?

Sure, there are challenges. Some folks in the informal sector might be wary of change, or they might not even know how to go about becoming official. That's where the government and organizations come in – they need to make the process simple and easy to understand.

The Pakistan Dream

Think of it like this: formalization is an investment in Pakistan's future. It's about giving everyone a fair shot at success, no matter where they start. It's about building an economy that's strong, stable, and fair for everyone.

Let's Talk Numbers

GDP Boost: The informal sector is already a big player in Pakistan's economy. Formalization could make it even bigger, adding a serious chunk to the country's GDP.

Job Creation: As these businesses grow, they'll need to hire more people, creating even more jobs.

Tax Revenue: Formal businesses pay taxes, which means more money for the government to invest in things like healthcare, education, and infrastructure.

Social Impact: Formalization can help reduce poverty, empower women, and improve working conditions for millions.

The Time is Now

So, why haven't we done this already? Well, change is hard, and this kind of transformation takes time and effort. But it's not impossible. Other countries have done it, and Pakistan can too.

A Vision for the Future

Imagine a Pakistan where everyone has the chance to succeed, where hard work and innovation are rewarded, and where the economy is a force for good. That's the vision of formalization.

We're All in This Together

This isn't just a job for the government. We all have a role to play. As consumers, we can choose to support formal businesses. As citizens, we can demand better policies. And as a nation, we can work together to build a better future for all.

The Bottom Line

Formalizing Pakistan's informal sector isn't a luxury, it's a necessity. It's about unlocking the full potential of the economy, creating a more equitable society, and building a future that we can all be proud of.

So, let's get this done. It's time for Pakistan to step up and show the world what it's truly capable of.

Alright folks, gather around! Let's chat about Pakistan. Not the usual stuff about politics or cricket, but something even cooler – technology. Yeah, you heard me right. Technology is shaking things up in Pakistan, big time. And it's not just about the latest gadgets, it's about a whole new way of doing business, growing the economy, and even changing society.

The Tech Tsunami

Picture this: tech wizards coding away in bustling cities, innovative farmers using data to grow better crops, and savvy entrepreneurs selling their crafts online to customers around the world. This is Pakistan today. Tech is like this awesome wave, washing over every corner of the country and bringing with it a tide of new possibilities.

Banking for Everyone

Let's start with banking. Ever heard of fintech? It's short for financial technology, and it's making banking way cooler. Now, folks in remote villages who never had a bank account can use their phones to send money, pay bills, and even get loans. This isn't just about convenience, it's about giving everyone a fair shot at financial security.

Farming Goes Digital

Next up, agriculture. Pakistan's always been an agricultural power-house, but now things are getting even more interesting. Farmers are using fancy tech like drones and data analytics to figure out the best time to plant, water, and harvest their crops. This means more food on the table, and more money in farmers' pockets.

E-commerce Explosion

But wait, there's more! E-commerce is booming. Remember those small shops we talked about? Well, many of them are now online, selling everything from handmade clothes to delicious snacks to a global audience. This means more jobs, more choices for consumers, and a more connected economy.

Beyond GDP

Now, I know what you're thinking – this is all great for the economy, but what about regular people? Well, that's the beauty of it. This tech wave isn't just about boosting GDP, it's about making life better for everyone.

Jobs, Jobs, Jobs

First off, it's creating a ton of new jobs. Tech companies need coders, designers, and marketers. Farmers need people who know how to operate drones and analyze data. E-commerce businesses need customer service reps and delivery drivers. And these are just a few examples.

Skill Up

But it's not just about the number of jobs, it's also about the quality. These new tech jobs require new skills, so people are learning and growing professionally. This means a more educated and skilled workforce, which is good for the whole country.

Spreading the Wealth

Another cool thing is that tech can reach even the most remote parts of Pakistan. So, it's not just the big cities that are benefiting. Even small towns and villages are getting in on the action, which means a more balanced and inclusive economy.

Challenges Ahead

Now, I'm not gonna lie, there are some challenges. Internet access isn't always great, especially in rural areas. And the government needs to keep up, making sure there are laws and regulations that support this new tech-driven economy.

Pakistan 2.0

But despite these challenges, Pakistan is on the cusp of something truly special. We're talking about a new Pakistan, a Pakistan that's more innovative, more connected, and more prosperous than ever before.

Policy Power

The government has a big role to play here. They need to invest in infrastructure, like internet cables and cell towers. They also need to make sure the rules are fair and transparent, so everyone can participate in this new economy.

The People's Revolution

But it's not just about the government. We, the people, also have a role to play. We need to embrace this tech wave, learn new skills, and support businesses that are innovating and creating jobs.

The Ripple Effect

Think of it like this: each new tech business, each farmer using data, each person buying something online – it's all like a little ripple in a pond. And together, these ripples can create a wave of change that transforms the entire country.

A Vision for the Future

So, let's dream big. Imagine a Pakistan where every kid has access to the internet, where farmers use the latest technology to grow food, and where anyone with a good idea can start a business. That's the kind of future that technology can make possible.

Real-World Examples

You don't have to take my word for it. Just look around. There are already amazing examples of how technology is changing Pakistan for the better.

Fintech Heroes: Companies like Easypaisa and JazzCash are giving millions of people access to financial services, even if they live in remote areas.

Agri-Tech Innovators: Startups like Farmar and Ricult are using AI and machine learning to help farmers increase their yields and reduce waste.

E-commerce Giants: Platforms like Daraz and Yayvo are making it possible for small businesses to reach a massive audience and sell their products nationwide.

The Road Ahead

Of course, there's still a lot of work to be done. But the foundation is there, and the momentum is building. With the right support and a bit of good old-fashioned Pakistani ingenuity, there's no limit to what we can achieve.

So, What's Next?

Well, that's up to us. We can choose to embrace this tech revolution, or we can let it pass us by. We can choose to invest in our people and our infrastructure, or we can fall behind. The choice is ours.

The Pakistan We Deserve

I believe that Pakistan deserves a bright future, a future where everyone has the chance to succeed, where innovation thrives, and where technology is used for good. And I believe that this future is within our reach.

So, let's get to work. Let's build the Pakistan we deserve. A Pakistan that's not just a player in the global economy, but a leader. A Pakistan that's known for its innovation, its creativity, and its resilience. A Pakistan that's a beacon of hope for the region and the world.

Environmental Concerns

Pakistan is getting scorched by the sun, and it's not just the usual summer heat. This is climate change in action, folks, and it's happening right now, right here. We're talking soaring temperatures, water disappearing like a mirage, and natural disasters hitting us harder and faster than ever before. It's a tough situation, especially for our communities who are already struggling.

Clean water, something we all take for granted, is becoming harder and harder to find in many parts of Pakistan. The wells are drying up, the rivers are shrinking, and that's making life tough for everyone, but especially those who are already living on the edge. It's not just about thirst either; it's about farming, it's about jobs, it's about survival.

The heat is brutal too. It's not just uncomfortable; it's causing serious health problems, particularly for the very young and the elderly. It's also making it harder to grow food. Our farmers are working tirelessly, but the scorching sun and lack of water are a constant battle. And as if that wasn't enough, we're also being hit by more and more natural disasters.

Floods, in particular, have become a terrifyingly regular occurrence. They come rushing in during the monsoon season, destroying everything in their path: homes, roads, crops. It's a heartbreaking sight, seeing families lose everything they have in an instant. And the worst part is, it's happening more often and with greater intensity every year. These floods are like a bully, always coming back to cause more pain and suffering.

It's a bleak picture, I know. But it's important to understand the reality of what's happening in Pakistan. Climate change is not some distant threat; it's a clear and present danger that's affecting us right now. And it's hitting hardest those who are already struggling to make ends meet.

Now, let's get into the nitty-gritty of how climate change is messing with Pakistan's environment. According to a study by Z Shahid and A Piracha (2010), the rising temperatures are a major culprit. They're like a villain in a comic book, causing all sorts of trouble. First, they're making our water disappear faster than a popsicle on a hot day. This is because the heat is causing more evaporation, both from rivers and from the ground. And when there's less water around, it's a big problem for everyone, especially for farmers who need it to grow our food.

The rising temperatures are also having a direct impact on our agriculture. It's like trying to bake a cake in an oven that's too hot; things just don't turn out right. Crops wither and die, harvests are smaller, and farmers are struggling to make ends meet. And this is a big deal in a country like Pakistan where so many people rely on agriculture for their livelihoods.

But it's not just about the heat and the lack of water. Climate change is also making our weather more unpredictable and extreme. It's like a roller coaster that's gone haywire, with sudden changes in temperature, unexpected droughts, and torrential downpours. And as we all know, these extreme weather events can be deadly, especially in a country like Pakistan where many people live in vulnerable housing and lack access to basic resources.

Take floods, for example. They've always been a part of life in Pakistan, but they're becoming more frequent and more intense due to climate change. It's like a monster that's getting bigger and stronger with each passing year. These floods destroy homes, crops, and infrastructure, leaving communities in ruins. And they can also lead to the spread of waterborne diseases, putting even more lives at risk.

So, what can we do about this? We can't just sit around and wait for the next disaster to strike. We need to take action now, and we need to take action together. We need to invest in climate-resilient infrastructure, develop sustainable water management practices, and support our farmers in adapting to the changing climate. We also need to raise awareness about the impacts of climate change and educate people on how to prepare for and respond to natural disasters.

It's a daunting challenge, but we can't give up hope. We need to be resilient, just like the people of Pakistan have always been. We need to adapt, innovate, and find new ways to thrive in this changing world. And we need to do it together, because we're all in this boat together. The future of our country, our communities, and our planet depends on it.

So, let's roll up our sleeves and get to work. Let's show the world what Pakistan is made of. Let's build a brighter, more sustainable future for ourselves and for generations to come.

Hey there, let's chat about how Pakistan is stepping up its game in protecting its incredible biodiversity. We're not just talking about the usual tree-hugging stuff here; we're talking cutting-edge technology, community teamwork, and a whole lot of passion for nature.

Imagine this: satellite imagery and drones swooping over lush land-scapes, keeping an eye on wildlife like some high-tech nature documen-tary. It's happening in Pakistan's protected areas, where these gadgets help rangers catch poachers and keep tabs on our precious animal popu-lations. It's like a superhero team, with technology as their superpower, fighting to preserve our natural treasures.

But technology is just one piece of the puzzle. Pakistan has also real-ized that the heart of conservation lies in the hands of its people. That's why they've launched all sorts of community-based projects, where local folks are learning how to protect their environment while also earning a living. It's like a win-win situation, where nature thrives and communi-ties prosper.

These local communities aren't just following orders from scientists; they're bringing their own wisdom to the table. They've been living in harmony with nature for generations, and they know a thing or two about sustainable practices. So, it's like a blend of ancient wisdom and modern science, working together to create a recipe for a healthy ecosys-tem.

Of course, Pakistan hasn't forgotten the basics. They've established national parks and wildlife reserves all across the country, like safe havens for endangered species. These protected areas aren't just pretty to look at; they're crucial for maintaining healthy populations of all sorts of creatures, from majestic snow leopards to tiny butterflies.

But even with all this good stuff happening, there have been chal-lenges along the way. Some communities were initially hesitant to em-brace conservation efforts, perhaps fearing it would disrupt their way of life. But organizations like WWF-Pakistan have been working tire-lessly to bridge the gap, engaging with local people and showing them the benefits of protecting their environment.

For instance, in some villages, WWF-Pakistan teamed up with the locals to create eco-tourism projects. This not only generates income for the community but also raises awareness about the importance of preserving their natural surroundings. It's like turning nature into a business, where everyone gets a share of the profits.

The use of technology has also faced some hurdles. Getting accurate data on wildlife populations and tracking illegal activities in vast, remote areas is no easy feat. But through constant innovation and collaboration with experts from around the world, Pakistan is finding ways to overcome these challenges.

In the end, it's the combination of all these efforts that makes Pakistan's approach to biodiversity conservation so unique and effective. It's not just about the government or the scientists; it's about everyone working together to protect our natural heritage. It's about respecting the wisdom of local communities, embracing new technologies, and finding creative ways to live in harmony with nature.

The road to effective biodiversity conservation is long and winding, with plenty of bumps along the way. But Pakistan is showing us that it's a journey worth taking. It's a journey that requires dedication, ingenuity, and a whole lot of heart. But the reward is a healthier planet, a richer culture, and a brighter future for generations to come.

Hey there, let's dive into the deep end of Pakistan's water woes. It's a complicated situation, like a tangled knot of problems all twisted together. We're talking serious water shortages, pollution that's making our rivers sick, and people fighting over the few drops that are left. It's not a pretty picture, but it's one we need to face head-on.

First things first, we can't just slap on a Band-Aid and call it a day. We need a real solution, something that gets to the root of the problem. That's where something called Integrated Water Resource Management (IWRM) comes in. It's like a big puzzle where we fit together all the different ways we use water – for farming, for industry, for our homes – and make sure everyone gets their fair share without ruining the environment. It's a team effort, folks, and everyone needs to play their part.

But even with the best management in the world, we still have a big problem: pollution. Our rivers, especially the mighty Indus, are being choked by all sorts of nasty stuff. It's like someone dumped a whole bunch of trash in our bathtub. That's why we need to invest in some serious water cleaning tech. Think of it like a super-powered filter that can take even the dirtiest water and make it safe to drink.

And here's the thing, we can't just rely on the government or some fancy tech to solve this problem. We need everyone to pitch in. That means educating people about why water is so precious, and how we can all use it more wisely. It means getting local communities involved in managing their own water resources, so they have a say in how it's used and protected. It's like a neighborhood watch, but for water.

Now, some folks might say, "Why bother with all this fancy stuff? Let's just build more dams and reservoirs." And sure, storing more water is important, but it's not the whole answer. If we just hoard water without dealing with pollution and overuse, it's like trying to fill a leaky bucket. We need to tackle all these problems together, like a team of superheroes with different powers.

Let me give you an example. Imagine a village in rural Pakistan that's struggling with water shortages. They've been relying on a nearby river, but it's been getting polluted and drying up. Now, imagine a group of experts comes in and helps them build a small dam to collect rainwater.

They also show them how to use less water for irrigation and install filters to clean the river water. And the villagers themselves form a committee to manage the water resources and make sure everyone gets their fair share.

This is what IWRM is all about. It's not just about the big projects, but also about the small, everyday actions that can make a real difference. It's about empowering communities to take control of their own water future, and it's about using technology to protect our precious resources.

So, where do we go from here? Well, it's not going to be easy. It's going to take a lot of hard work, collaboration, and investment. But the good news is, we already have the tools and the knowledge to make it happen. We just need the will.

Pakistan is a country with a rich history and a bright future. We've overcome challenges before, and we can overcome this one too. But it's going to take all of us working together, like a family, to protect our water, our environment, and our way of life. It's not just about us; it's about our children and grandchildren, and the kind of world we want to leave them.

So, let's roll up our sleeves, put our heads together, and start building a better water future for Pakistan. Let's show the world that we can rise to the challenge and create a model for sustainable water management. The time for action is now.

Hey there, let's have a chat about the exciting things happening in Pakistan regarding our environment. It's like a green revolution is sweeping through the nation, and it's pretty inspiring to see. People from all walks of life are stepping up to make Pakistan a more eco-friendly place, and they're doing it in some really innovative ways.

Ever heard of the Billion Tree Tsunami? No, it's not a natural disaster, but a massive campaign to plant billions of trees across the country. It's like a green army is marching across the land, combating deforestation and breathing new life into our forests. And these trees aren't just pretty to look at; they're helping to clean our air, conserve water, and provide habitat for all sorts of creatures. It's a win-win for everyone, from the smallest insects to the largest mammals, and of course, us humans too!

But it's not just about planting trees. Pakistanis are getting creative with eco-friendly practices in all sorts of areas. Our farmers, for instance, are increasingly turning to organic methods. That means ditching the harmful chemicals and embracing natural ways to grow food. It's better for the soil, it's better for the crops, and it's definitely better for our health.

And it doesn't stop at the farms. Even our industries are jumping on the green bandwagon. You'll find factories using renewable energy like solar and wind power, which is like harnessing the power of the sun and wind to run their machines. It's a cleaner, greener way to do business, and it's helping to reduce our carbon footprint.

Even the way we deal with waste is changing. More and more companies are finding ways to recycle and reuse materials, so less ends up in landfills. It's like giving trash a second life, turning it into something useful instead of just throwing it away.

Now, you might be wondering, "What's behind all this green enthusiasm?" Well, it's a combination of things. For one, people are becoming more aware of the environmental challenges facing our planet, from climate change to pollution. And they're realizing that we need to take action now before it's too late.

But it's not just about fear or guilt. It's also about hope and optimism. People are seeing that we can make a difference, that we can create a better future for ourselves and our children. And they're eager to be part of the solution.

Of course, it's not all smooth sailing. There are still challenges to overcome. Changing old habits and adopting new practices can be difficult, especially when it comes to industries that have been doing things a certain way for a long time.

But here's the exciting part: we're seeing a real shift in mindset. More and more people are embracing environmental responsibility, not just as a duty, but as a way of life. It's becoming cool to be green, and that's a powerful thing.

This cultural shift is being driven by a number of factors. Educational institutions are playing a key role, teaching young people about the importance of sustainability. NGOs are also getting involved, organizing workshops and awareness campaigns to reach a wider audience.

And it's not just the younger generation that's getting on board. Even our corporate sector is stepping up. Many companies are now incorporating sustainability into their business models, not just because it's the right thing to do, but because it makes good business sense. After all, a healthy planet means a healthy economy.

We're seeing companies investing in green technologies, reducing their waste, and supporting environmental initiatives in their communities. It's a win-win situation, where businesses can thrive while also contributing to a better future for all.

So, what's the takeaway from all of this? Well, I think it's safe to say that Pakistan is on the right track when it comes to environmental sustainability. We're not perfect, and there's still a long way to go. But the progress we've made so far is encouraging, and it gives us hope for the future.

It's a reminder that even small actions can have a big impact, and that we all have a role to play in protecting our planet. Whether it's planting a tree, recycling, or supporting eco-friendly businesses, every little bit helps.

So, let's keep the momentum going. Let's continue to embrace green initiatives, both big and small. Let's show the world that Pakistan is committed to building a more sustainable future for all. Because at the end of the day, we're not just doing this for ourselves; we're doing it for the generations to come.

Technological Advancements

Imagine stepping back in time to ancient Pakistan. The scene you'd encounter might surprise you: bustling cities with well-organized streets, complex plumbing systems that would make a modern city planner proud, and bustling port filled with ships guided by the stars. Sounds a bit like a sci-fi movie, doesn't it? But this wasn't a fantasy – it was real life for the people of the Indus Valley Civilization and later, the Mughal Empire.

Let's start our journey in the Indus Valley, way back around 2600 BC. This civilization was light-years ahead of its time when it came to city planning. Their streets weren't just random paths – they were laid out in a grid pattern, kind of like modern city blocks. And forget about stinky open sewers – these folks had covered drains and even toilets in some homes! All of this made their cities clean, healthy places to live, attracting people from far and wide to trade and settle down.

These ingenious people weren't just good at building cities; they were also fantastic farmers. They created intricate irrigation systems that channeled water exactly where it was needed, ensuring bumper crops even during dry spells. This agricultural know-how was a major factor in the Indus Valley's economic success.

Fast forward a few millennia to the Mughal Empire, and you'll find another wave of incredible innovation. The Mughals took irrigation to the next level, introducing new techniques and expanding existing systems. They also introduced new crops to the region, like maize and chili peppers (ever had a spicy biryani? You can thank the Mughals for that!).

The Mughal emperors weren't just interested in agriculture; they were also patrons of science and the arts. They supported the development of amazing tools like the astrolabe, which was used to measure the position of stars and planets. This was a game-changer for navigation, making sea voyages safer and more reliable. In turn, this boosted trade and led to more cultural exchange with neighboring regions.

Think of the Mughals as the Renaissance men of their time: they were curious about everything from astronomy to architecture. This intellectual curiosity fueled a period of incredible creativity and innovation, impacting everything from art and literature to technology.

Now, you might be wondering what all of this has to do with modern-day Pakistan. Well, the answer is simple: these historical innovations laid the groundwork for the country we know today. The Indus Valley Civilization showed us how to build thriving cities, while the Mughals taught us the importance of agricultural innovation and scientific inquiry.

Take small businesses in Pakistan, for example. They often draw inspiration from these historical traditions of innovation and collaboration. Just like the Mughal emperors encouraged knowledge sharing, modern Pakistani entrepreneurs often work together to create new products and services. This spirit of open innovation has helped to drive economic growth and create jobs.

And the spirit of innovation is still alive and well in Pakistan today. From cutting-edge tech startups to grassroots social enterprises, Pakistanis are constantly finding new ways to solve problems and make their communities better.

So the next time you stroll down a busy street in Karachi or Lahore, remember: you're walking in the footsteps of innovators who lived thousands of years ago. The legacy of their creativity and ingenuity is still shaping Pakistan today, inspiring future generations to build an even brighter tomorrow.

It's pretty amazing to think about how these historical innovations have impacted everything from our food to our technology. And who knows what amazing things the future holds? One thing's for sure: with its rich history of innovation, Pakistan is well-positioned to continue making its mark on the world stage.

Pakistan is like a tech-savvy phoenix rising from the ashes. It's not just about catching up anymore; it's about leading the charge. From the bustling tech hubs in Lahore to the cutting-edge biotech labs in Karachi, Pakistan is rewriting its narrative with each technological stride.

Think of it as a symphony of innovation. The IT sector is hitting all the right notes, booming with software development and outsourcing opportunities. It's become this magnet for international investment, and it's not hard to see why. The talent here is top-notch, and the ambition is through the roof.

But wait, there's more! Biotechnology is another melody in this symphony, and it's playing a tune of progress. Scientists are hard at work, making groundbreaking discoveries that could change the game for agriculture and healthcare. Imagine farmers with super-resilient crops and doctors armed with new treatments for diseases that were once thought incurable. That's the potential we're talking about.

And what about the grand finale of this symphony? It's the breath-taking ascent into space exploration. Pakistan is determined to join the exclusive club of spacefaring nations, and it's not just about national pride. It's about technological independence and a seat at the table of global space initiatives.

This isn't just about fancy gadgets and space rockets, though. This technological transformation is weaving a new economic fabric for Pakistan. It's creating jobs, attracting investment, and boosting industries across the board. The government's "Pakistan Vision" policy document is like the conductor's baton, guiding this symphony of progress.

But here's the thing: Pakistan isn't just playing for a domestic audience. It's got its sights set on the global stage. And the world is starting to take notice. Experts and investors are recognizing Pakistan as a rising star in the tech world.

This is where things get really exciting. Pakistan isn't just adopting new technologies; it's adapting them to its unique challenges and opportunities. For example, they're using blockchain technology to crack down on financial crime like money laundering. Who knew fighting crime could be so high-tech?

And it's not just about the big stuff either. Even small businesses are getting in on the action. The spirit of collaboration is alive and well, with knowledge-sharing and partnerships paving the way for innovation at all levels.

Of course, with all this progress comes a responsibility to do things right. Pakistan is taking a holistic approach, focusing on sustainable practices and ensuring that everyone benefits from this technological revolution.

This means more than just shiny new gadgets. It's about education, policy, and building a skilled workforce that can carry this momentum forward. It's about ensuring that this progress is inclusive and equitable, so that everyone has a chance to thrive in this new era.

Now, some might say this is all too good to be true. They might point to challenges and obstacles that Pakistan still faces. But that's missing the bigger picture. This isn't just about solving problems; it's about creating opportunities.

Think of it like a rocket launch. There's a lot of preparation, a lot of fuel to burn, and a lot of potential for things to go wrong. But when that rocket finally takes off, it's a sight to behold. That's where Pakistan is right now – poised for takeoff, with the potential to reach new heights.

So, what's the takeaway? Pakistan is in the midst of a technological revolution, and it's not just changing the country's economy; it's changing its identity. It's a story of ambition, innovation, and a determination to make a mark on the world. It's a story that's still being written, but one thing's for sure: it's a story worth paying attention to.

Picture this: Pakistan, a country known for its rich history and vibrant culture, is now buzzing with a new kind of energy – the energy of innovation. It's like the country has found its entrepreneurial groove, and it's not slowing down anytime soon.

At the heart of this excitement are the startups and the research institutions, working together like a dynamic duo. These startups are like the new kids on the block, full of fresh ideas and a hunger to change the world. Meanwhile, the research institutions are like the wise elders, providing the knowledge and expertise to help those ideas take flight.

Think of it like a relay race: the research institutions pass the baton of knowledge to the startups, who then sprint towards innovation, creating new products, services, and solutions that are making life better for people across Pakistan and beyond.

But it's not just about the startups and researchers doing their thing. The government and the private sector are playing a crucial role in making all this happen. They've realized that if they want Pakistan to thrive in the 21st century, they need to invest in innovation.

So, they've launched a whole bunch of initiatives to help startups get off the ground. Think of it like a support system for entrepreneurs: there's funding to help them get started, mentorship to guide them along the way, and opportunities to collaborate with others and share ideas. It's like a recipe for success, with all the right ingredients in place.

And it's not just talk; it's actually working. There are success stories all over the country – startups that have taken advantage of these initiatives and turned their dreams into reality. Take ChallengeX Pakistan, for example. It's a startup competition that gives young entrepreneurs the chance to pitch their ideas and get the support they need to bring their products to market. It's like a talent show for innovators, where the prize is a chance to change the world.

Then there are the incubation centers, where startups can rent affordable office space, get access to resources and equipment, and network with other entrepreneurs. It's like a co-working space on steroids, designed specifically to help startups grow and succeed.

The beauty of this innovation ecosystem is that it's not just about making money. It's about solving real-world problems and making a positive impact on society. Startups are tackling everything from healthcare to education to climate change, using technology to create solutions that are both innovative and sustainable.

And it's not just happening in big cities like Karachi and Lahore. Innovation is spreading to all corners of the country, as entrepreneurs in smaller towns and rural areas are getting in on the action. This is where the research institutions come in, working with local communities to identify challenges and develop solutions that are tailored to their specific needs.

The collaboration between academia and industry is another key ingredient in this recipe for success. Research institutions are working with startups to translate academic knowledge into practical applications. It's like bridging the gap between theory and practice, creating a virtuous cycle where research leads to innovation, which then leads to more research.

But it's not all smooth sailing. Startups still face challenges, like access to funding and navigating complex regulations. But the government and the private sector are working to address these issues, creating a more conducive environment for innovation to flourish.

So, what does the future hold for Pakistan's innovation landscape? It's hard to say for sure, but one thing is clear: the momentum is building. With a growing pool of talented entrepreneurs, supportive institutions, and a government that's committed to fostering innovation, Pakistan is poised to become a major player in the global tech scene.

Think of it as a story that's just beginning. It's a story about a country that's embracing technology and using it to create a brighter future for its people. It's a story about collaboration, creativity, and the power of human ingenuity to overcome challenges and create positive change. And it's a story that's inspiring people all over the world.

Picture this: Pakistan, a land of vibrant culture and immense potential, is stepping onto the global tech stage, ready to dance. But it's not just a casual waltz; this is more like a high-energy bhangra performance, fueled by a desire to transform challenges into triumphs.

Now, Pakistan isn't exactly starting from scratch. They've got some serious hurdles to jump, like patchy internet access and a wide gap between the haves and have-nots. It's like trying to run a marathon with a sprained ankle. But here's the twist: Pakistan is using those very challenges as fuel for its innovative fire.

Think of it like a classic underdog story. Everyone loves rooting for the team that's not supposed to win, right? Well, Pakistan is that team, and they're proving that sometimes, it's the underdogs who have the most to gain.

Let's talk about the challenges first. Not everyone has access to high-speed internet, especially in rural areas. And even in the cities, there's a huge gap between the tech-savvy elite and those who are still catching up. It's like having a fancy sports car but no roads to drive it on.

But hold on a minute. Challenges aren't always a bad thing. They can spark creativity and force you to think outside the box. In Pakistan's case, these challenges have become a driving force for innovation.

Take digital infrastructure, for example. The lack of reliable internet in some areas has actually spurred the development of creative solutions, like solar-powered Wi-Fi hotspots and mobile internet vans that bring connectivity to remote villages. It's like building a bridge where there was none before.

Education is another area where Pakistan is turning challenges into opportunities. While traditional teaching methods might not be cutting it in the digital age, educators are finding new ways to engage students and prepare them for the future. They're incorporating technology into classrooms, creating online courses, and even using virtual reality to bring lessons to life.

But innovation isn't just happening in classrooms and tech labs. It's happening in everyday life, too. Entrepreneurs are using technology to solve problems that have plagued Pakistan for years, like access to clean water, affordable healthcare, and financial services for the unbanked.

Think of it like a ripple effect. One small innovation can lead to another, and another, until it creates a wave of change that washes over the entire country. And that's exactly what's happening in Pakistan.

Of course, none of this happens overnight. It takes time, effort, and a whole lot of collaboration. The government, the private sector, educational institutions, and everyday citizens all have a role to play. It's like a team sport, where everyone needs to work together to score that winning goal.

The government is setting the stage by creating policies that encourage innovation and investment. They're providing funding for startups, streamlining regulations, and creating a business environment that's conducive to growth. It's like giving the team a pep talk and a playbook to follow.

Meanwhile, the private sector is stepping up to the plate with funding, mentorship, and infrastructure. They're creating incubators and accelerators that help startups get off the ground and providing training programs to develop the next generation of tech talent. It's like providing the team with the best equipment and coaches.

And then there are the educational institutions, the unsung heroes of this story. They're the ones who are educating and training the workforce that will drive Pakistan's digital future. They're partnering with industry to ensure that students have the skills they need to succeed in a rapidly changing world. It's like creating a farm team of future stars.

But it's not just about the big players. Everyday citizens are also getting involved, using their creativity and ingenuity to solve problems in their communities. They're starting businesses, developing apps, and using technology to make a difference in their own lives and the lives of others. It's like a grassroots movement, powered by the collective energy of the Pakistani people.

So, what does the future hold for Pakistan's tech scene? It's hard to say for sure, but one thing's clear: the potential is immense. With a young, tech-savvy population, a supportive government, and a growing number of innovative startups, Pakistan is well-positioned to become a major player in the global digital economy.

Think of it as a marathon, not a sprint. There will be challenges along the way, but with the right mindset and the right support, Pakistan can overcome those challenges and reach the finish line. And when it does, the whole world will be watching.

This bestselling author combines financial expertise (ACCA, MBA) with proven technical skills (Google certifications) to deliver insightful books. With ten years of business experience.

www.ingramcontent.com/pod-product-compliance
Ingram Content Group UK Ltd.
Pitfield, Milton Keynes, MK11 3LW, UK
UKHW040747270125
454275UK00006B/348

9 783384 464491